D1646823

San Francisco

Select

contents

San Francisco overview

'San Francisco is 49 square miles surrounded by reality' Paul Kantner, Jefferson Airplane

Although it's actually 47 square miles, Kantner nailed it. This city of 43 hills on the edge of the continent, separated from the rest of the world on three sides by glittering water, is a place of staggering beauty, rich ethnic diversity, a laidback attitude, and more than a touch of quirk.

San Francisco was born of a pioneer spirit – miners flocked here to find their fortunes during the California Gold Rush of 1849, and the debauchery of the Barbary Coast is the stuff of legend. The city has always attracted eccentrics and entrepreneurs, dreamers and doers. The legacy of the Beats in the 1950s, and then the rabblerousing hippies of the '60s, is an enduring bohemia, a welcoming place to artists and oddballs, and a safe haven for alternative lifestyles.

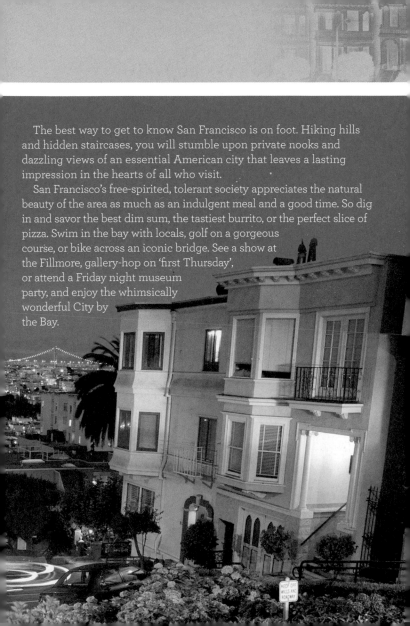

The best way to get to know San Francisco is on foot. Hiking hills and hidden staircases, you will stumble upon private nooks and dazzling views of an essential American city that leaves a lasting impression in the hearts of all who visit.

San Francisco's free-spirited, tolerant society appreciates the natural beauty of the area as much as an indulgent meal and a good time. So dig in and savor the best dim sum, the tastiest burrito, or the perfect slice of pizza. Swim in the bay with locals, golf on a gorgeous course, or bike across an iconic bridge. See a show at the Fillmore, gallery-hop on 'first Thursday', or attend a Friday night museum party, and enjoy the whimsically wonderful City by the Bay.

KEEP OFF
WALLS AND
ROADWAY

in the mood for...

... romance

Tony Bennett left his heart here, and it is easy to see why. A city of tremendous views, hidden corners, cozy accommodations, and fine food, San Francisco pulses with romance. Stroll along the windswept coast beneath fragrant eucalyptus at **Land's End** *(p.160)* and gaze at sunset over the Pacific or the **Golden Gate Bridge** *(p.156)* silhouetted by fog. Across town, pick up a bottle of sparkling wine and some snacks and ferret out tiny **Jack Early Park** *(p.37)* for a private picnic before settling into the corner turret suite at **Washington Square Inn** *(p.178)*. You can take the chill off a San Francisco night snuggling by the fireplace in your room at the **White Swan Inn** *(p.178)*. And for memorable and romantic meals, go French. Share savory and sweet soufflés at intimate **Café Jacqueline** *(p.37)*, or try classic French cuisine in the sumptuous fabric-draped dining room at **Fleur de Lys** *(p.72)*.

.... fine dining

San Franciscans are passionate about food. A multiethnic town that pushes the creative envelope and is on the vanguard of culinary movements, it has an established place at the global table.

To see this food fetish in action, visit the **Ferry Building Marketplace** *(p.74)*. At this epicurean shrine, you can slurp freshly shucked oysters at Hog Island, nibble almost-too-pretty-to-eat chocolates at Recchiuiti, and savor sublime cheese at Cowgirl Creamery.

California cuisine changed the culinary world. You can taste the revolution at many local restaurants, including **Boulevard** *(p.90)*, **Foreign Cinema** *(p.142)*, and **Nopa** *(p.107)* – all adherents of the philosophy of using seasonal, locally produced, organic ingredients. But the ultimate gastronomic orgy is at **Gary Danko** *(p.29)*. The five-course tasting menu includes optional wine pairings and a cheese cart, and offers perfectly executed food that bursts with flavor and is nothing short of art.

... literary inspiration

To immerse yourself in San Francisco's literary scene, start at **Caffe Trieste** (*p.33*) or **Vesuvio** (*p.40*), two favorite haunts of the Beat Generation writers, then catch a reading at **City Lights Booksellers** (*p.40*). From here, climb Russian Hill to glimpse the house where Kerouac worked on notes for *On the Road* (*p.40*) or meander down **Macondray Lane** (*p.52*), the inspiration for Armistead Maupin's Barbary Lane in *Tales of the City*.

Over in Alamo Square, you can view the pristinely preserved Victorian **Westerfield House** (*p.109*), a former flophouse described by Tom Wolfe in *The Electric Kool-Aid Acid Test*.

Devotees of Dashiell Hammett, who used San Francisco as a backdrop in his series of detective novels that include *The Maltese Falcon*, can book a charming suite dedicated to the scribe at **Hotel Union Square** (*p.170*).

A sojourn to **826 Valencia**, Dave Eggers' pirate-store-meets-writing-center (*p.137*), is mandatory for postmodern literature buffs. And no bibliophile should miss funky **Green Apple Books** (*p.158*), beloved by locals.

... being pampered

For the ultimate in pampering, head to the **Nob Hill Spa** (*p.56*). Make a day of it and relax on the sundeck or by the pool with lunch and a drink. Rejuvenate in the steam room, sauna, and tubs at the Japanese-style baths of **Kabuki Springs & Spa** (*p.104*).

For a quick pick-me-up, there is nothing like a foot massage. Reflexology at Chinatown's **Lucky Foot Massage** (*p.50*) will rock your socks off. A full menu of wellness services awaits at **Senspa** (*p.154*), uniquely located in a former army barracks.

... a quintessential experience

Start with an Irish coffee at **Buena Vista**, then hop on the cable car out front (*p.27*). Jump off at the top of Russian Hill, meander down the curves of **Lombard Street** (*p.51*), then hike up to **Coit Tower** (*p.34*) on Telegraph Hill. Enjoy crab or cioppino (a San Francisco fish stew) for lunch at **Tadich Grill** (*p.71*), and squeeze in a tour of the **Anchor Brewing Company** (*p.167*) before heading out on the bay for a night tour of **Alcatraz** (*p.26*).

... a bohemian atmosphere

San Francisco's bohemian flavor can trace its roots to the free-spirited Beat writers. Get hip to that scene at the **Beat Museum** *(p.41)* in North Beach, then make your way across town and groove to a percussion jam at **Hippie Hill** *(p.125)* and see the boho spirit alive and well in hippie counterculture. Stop for retro gear on **Haight Street** *(p.122)*, then catch a show at the **Fillmore Auditorium** *(p.103)*, or immerse yourself in the new bohemia through a bar crawl of the **Mission** *(p.140)*.

... escaping the crowds

One of San Francisco's greatest assets is its proximity to nature, offering quiet corners for escape. In Golden Gate Park, walk up **Strawberry Hill** *(p.126)* over stone bridges and past a waterfall or slip into one of many peaceful gardens *(p.128)*. Explore **Buena Vista Park** *(p.117)* for tranquil respite in the middle of the city. With 22 hiking trails in nearly 1,500 acres, it is easy to find a peaceful, private nook in the **Presidio** *(p.154)*.

... family fun

Child-friendly San Francisco has plenty of options to occupy young bodies and minds. Kids love **Fisherman's Wharf** *(p.31)*, with its **Musee Mechanique** and the **USS** *Pampanito*, a World War II fleet submarine.

The **Exploratorium** *(p.100)* is a crowd-pleaser, with hands-on science exhibits. Teenagers will be inspired at **Zeum**, a hip multimedia museum *(p.85)*.

The city is dotted with great playgrounds, including **Julius Kahn** in the Presidio *(p.154)*. **Golden Gate Park** has an awesome playground with a carrousel *(p.125)*, the fascinating **California Academy of Sciences** *(p.124)* with a planetarium and an aquarium, and paddleboats at **Stow Lake** *(p.126)*. At the **San Francisco Zoo** *(p.166)* are a children's zoo and a steam train. When it's time for bed, **Hotel Metropolis** and **Hotel Union Square** both offer special kids' suites *(p.170)*.

... retail therapy

Pockets of retail can be found in boutique-lined neighborhoods all over the city, or you can shop beneath one roof in larger malls. **Maiden Lane** *(p.70)* is a shopper's paradise with designer couture boutiques and San Francisco institution Gumps. The **Westfield Centre** *(p.86)* has hundreds of shops, including department store Nordstrom.

Shop on **Haight Street** for **Amoeba Music** *(p.116)*, funky retro clothing, and thrift stores *(p.122)*. The **Mission** has one-of-a-kind shops like Paxton Gate and the Curiosity Shoppe *(p.137)*. Hip **Hayes Valley** *(p.110)* is good for shoes and modern fashions. A clutch of local designers on upper **Fillmore Street** *(p.102)* offer fashion-forward womenswear. **Jackson Square** is your go-to spot for antique browsing and Carrots *(p.73)*, a contemporary fashion emporium.

Eclectic **Clement Street** includes Green Apple Books *(p.158)*. Not to be overlooked are enclaves on **Polk Street** *(p.57)*, in **North Beach** *(p.36)*, and **Chinatown** *(p.50)*.

... great art

Each of the four big art museums has a distinct personality, unique architecture, and a diverse collection. Look for the oldest dated bronze Buddha at the **Asian Art Museum** (p.89), one of the world's most comprehensive Asian art collections. Find a trove of American and African art at the **de Young** (p.127) and marvel at the copper-clad building. **SFMOMA**'s (p.80) collection includes Dalí, Rothko, Pollock, and Steiglitz. The regal **Palace of the Legion of Honor** (p.163) showcases Rodin sculptures and paintings by European masters.

... being active

A mild climate makes it easy to get active here, and there is no shortage of things to do, from walking to windsurfing. Climbing steep hills and **staircases** (p.52) can qualify as a workout, but why not rent a bike and ride across the landmark **Golden Gate Bridge** (p.156)? You can golf on a scenic course (p.161), go lawn bowling or play archery in **Golden Gate Park** (p.130), jog in the **Presidio** (p.154), or take a refreshing swim in the bay at **Fisherman's Wharf** (p.29).

... street life

In North Beach, the cafes along **Columbus Avenue** *(p.33)* are ideal for watching an international cross-section of people amble by. The Castro Street area thrives day and night – grab an outdoor table at **Café Flore** *(p.149)* for the most intriguing people watching in town. Punks, hippies and trust-fund kids begging for change congregate on the **Haight** – see them in action over breakfast *(p.120)*. Hipsters roam Valencia and Mission Streets, while deeper in the neighborhood on **24th Street** *(p.143)* is a largely Hispanic crowd and an explosion of street mural art.

Busy Chinatown streets are a colorful cultural experience by day and take skill to weave through. Pretty people and foodie folks pop up on Saturday mornings at the **Ferry Building Farmers Market** *(p.75)*, and a sophisticated nighttime scene is found in the **French Quarter** on Belden Place *(p.72)*.

... architecture

Fans of Victorian architecture should start at **Alamo Square** by viewing the Painted Ladies, and around the corner, the remarkable **Westerfield House** (p.108–9). Many more examples of Victorian and Edwardian houses are found here and in neighboring Haight-Ashbury and Pacific Heights. You can take an educational tour of the **Haas-Lilienthal House** (p.109) or spend the night at the **Red Victorian** (p.174), the **Hotel Majestic** (p.178), or the **Chateau Tivoli** (p.108).

The Streamline Moderne buildings in **Aquatic Park** (p.28) are a must-see for Art Deco-lovers, before moving on to **Chestnut Street** in the Marina (p.99). Have dinner at the Deco **Beach Chalet** (p.131), then repair to the nautical-style **Ocean Park Motel** (p.175).

There are also great examples of modern and re-use architecture in the city, like the **InterContinental** (p.172), **SFMOMA** (p.80), the **Asian Art Museum** (p.89), and the **Contemporary Jewish Museum** (p.83).

... a night on the town

After dark, San Francisco becomes an adult playground with something for everyone. You can see live music at historic venues, international DJs at gay clubs, Broadway plays, or alternative theater and comedy.

If you are looking for a night of barhopping, the city is happy to oblige – the best neighborhoods for bars are the **Mission** *(p.140)*, **Haight Street** *(p.118)*, **NoPa** *(p.107)* and **North Beach**. Don't miss the great dive bars in **Chinatown** *(p.47)* – or for a very different experience, go on a hotel barhop in elegant **Nob Hill** *(p.53)*.

The **Fillmore** *(p.103)* and the **Warfield** *(p.67)* host major headliners. For indie bands try the Great American Music Hall *(p.67)*.

The **Mission** and **Castro** both have great places to dance, and there are some big nightclubs over in **SoMa** *(p.147)*.

Major mainstream theaters are near Union Square *(p.65)*, but for edgier material, try the alternative theaters in the **Mission** *(p.138)* or the **Magic Theatre** *(p.98)* at Fort Mason. Established comedy clubs are in and around **North Beach** *(p.38)*. Or catch a drag show at Kimo's *(p.57)*.

....history

For a primer on San Francisco history, begin at the **Mission Dolores** *(p.144)*, where the Franciscan Missionaries originally settled, then cross town to traipse through the old maritime neighborhoods on the **Barbary Coast Trail** *(p.64)*, for as much background as you can absorb. Once sufficiently educated, raise a glass to the Old West at the **Gold Dust Lounge** *(p.69)*, order from the old-school menu at **Sam's** *(p.71)*, and spend the night at **The Westin St Francis** *(p.172)*, steeped in Frisco history.

... something different

Tired of museums? Check out a sing-a-long at the **Castro Theatre** *(p.148)* – *Mary Poppins* is a fave. Need a spiritual lift? Walk the labyrinths at **Grace Cathedral** *(p.54)*, attend a jazz service at **St John Coltrane African Orthodox Church** *(p.106)*, or a Gospel celebration at **Glide** *(p.59)*. For Harajuku fashions and Japanese anime, head to **New People** *(p.105)*. Or for an unconventional cocktail experience, try **Bourbon & Branch** *(p.58)*.

neighborhoods

Extending from the San Francisco Bay in the east to the Pacific Ocean in the west, San Francisco is a city of neighborhoods, each with a distinct personality. Slicing diagonally across, Market Street divides much of the city by north and south.

Fisherman's Wharf and North Beach are two lively areas packed with attractions. The Wharf is congested and touristy, but in early morning or late evening you can get a sense of the original port city. Board the historic ships here and indulge in Dungeness crab. In the bustling Italian enclave of North Beach, soak up Barbary Coast and Beat Generation history from a sidewalk cafe or a barstool.

Chinatown, Russian Hill, and Nob Hill vary widely in character. Chinatown is cramped and colorful with fascinating alleys to explore, while Russian Hill is stylish and perfectly picturesque, and Nob Hill was the landing place of the city's original elite and still carries that cachet. The nearby Tenderloin neighborhood has pockets of beauty in an otherwise impoverished area.

Union Square and Financial District pulse with high heels and high-rises, department stores and couture designers, chic hotels and acclaimed restaurants, theatergoers and gallery-hoppers. Historic streetcars whizz by on Market Street as well-dressed businesspeople on smart phones plot their next moves.

SoMa and Civic Center are two separate experiences. SoMa (an acronym for South of Market) is home to several museums including SFMOMA, hotels, retail, and restaurants. It extends east to the Embarcadero and south to the Giants' ballpark. Civic Center is a cluster of regal Beaux-Arts buildings, including City Hall, the Symphony, and the Ballet, that are surrounded by seedy neighborhoods and a staggering amount of homelessness.

Central Neighborhoods comprise the neighborhoods west of Van Ness Avenue and east of Golden Gate Park. Get a glimpse of authentic San Francisco by shopping in the boutiques of local designers on Fillmore Street and in Hayes Valley, barhopping in NoPa, or immersing yourself in the city's architecture – Art Deco in the Marina and Victorian confections in Pacific Heights and Alamo Square. All deserve a trip off the beaten path.

Haight-Ashbury and Golden Gate Park lie to the south and west of the central 'hoods. 'The Haight' is the birthplace of the hippie counterculture. It retains a thriving nightlife, though many former crashpads are now inhabited by families. Beautiful Golden Gate Park is more than 1,000 lush acres of green, with top-flight museums, playgrounds, and quiet gardens.

Mission and Castro provide San Francisco's political and artistic edge. A Latino neighborhood embraced by the young and hip, the Mission is the center of the city's new bohemia and explodes with vibrant mural art. Next door, draped in rainbow-hued flags, the Castro is the gay capital of the world.

Outer Neighborhoods extend north and south of Golden Gate Park and south and west of the Mission. Here you can eat your way around the world at the ethnic restaurants of the Sunset and Richmond, visit beautiful beaches, hike through the pristine Presidio, or discover sunny Potrero Hill.

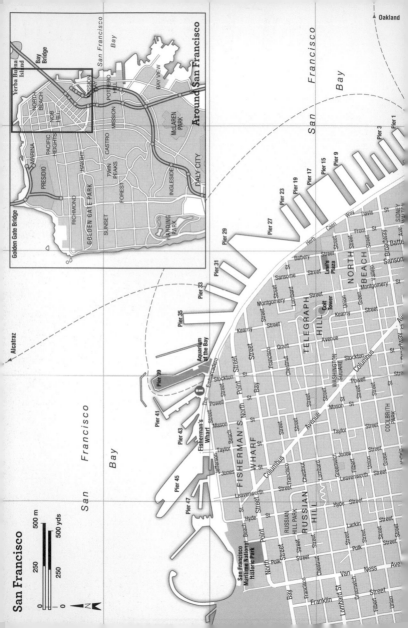

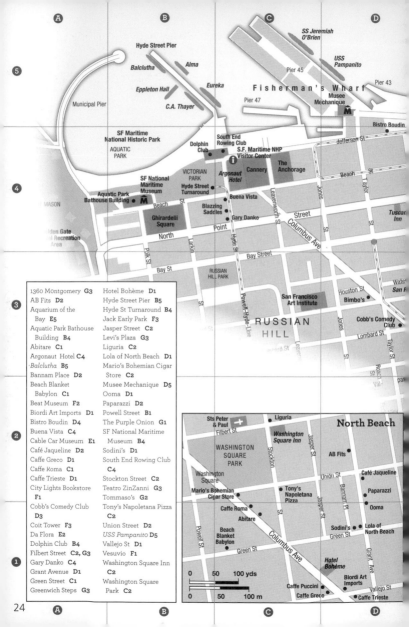

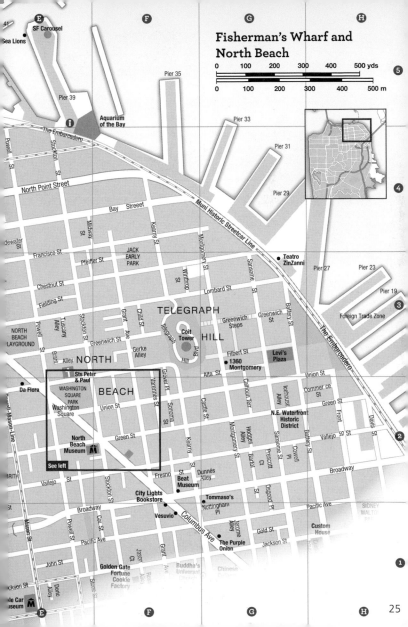

Fisherman's Wharf and North Beach

| 0 | 100 | 200 | 300 | 400 | 500 yds |
| 0 | 100 | 200 | 300 | 400 | 500 m |

Sea Lions

SF Carousel

Pier 35

Pier 39

Aquarium of the Bay

Pier 33

The Embarcadero

Powell St

Stockton St

Pier 31

Pier 29

North Point Street

Bay Street

Midway

Kearny St

Montgomery St

Sansome St

Muni Historic Streetcar Line

Teatro ZinZanni

Pier 27

Pier 23

Pier 19

Francisco St

Pfeiffer St

JACK EARLY PARK

Chestnut St

Winthrop St

Lombard St

Foreign Trade Zone

Fielding St

Tuscany Alley

Stockton St

Grant Ave

Child St

TELEGRAPH

Coit Tower

HILL

Greenwich Steps

Greenwich St

Battery St

The Embarcadero

NORTH BEACH PLAYGROUND

Powell St

Greenwich St

Gerke Alley

Telegraph Hill Blvd

Filbert St

1360 Montgomery

Levi's Plaza

Brant Alley

NORTH

Sts Peter & Paul

Alta St

Union St

Da Flora

WASHINGTON SQUARE PARK

Washington Square

BEACH

Varennes St

Sonoma St

Castle St

Calhoun Terr

Montgomery St

Icehouse Alley

Commerce St

N.E. Waterfront Historic District

Green St

Jason-Mason Line

North Beach Museum

Green St

Kearny St

Hodges Alley

Sansome St

Battery St

Prescott Ct

Cowell Pl

Vallejo St

Front St

Davis St

See left

BRITH

Vallejo St

Stockton St

Fresno St

St

Dunnes Alley

Beat Museum

Broadway

Broadway

City Lights Bookstore

Columbus Ave

Vesuvio

Tommaso's

Nottingham Pl

Osgood Pl

Pacific Ave

SIDNEY WALTO

Powell St

Cor. St

Grant Ave

The Purple Onion

Jerome Alley

Gold St

Jackson St

Custom House

Pacific Ave

John St

Golden Gate Fortune Cookie Factory

Jason Ave

Buddha's Universal

Chinese

Doric Alley

le Car seum

Jackson St

25

Take a spooky **night tour of Alcatraz**

A visit to 'The Rock,' the site of the former maximum-security Federal penitentiary turned tourist destination, is chilling even on a sunny afternoon – but as darkness falls during this intimate night tour, **Alcatraz** becomes perfectly eerie.

After witnessing the Golden Gate Bridge (*p.156*) silhouetted against sunset during a scenic ferry crossing, the group disembarks, is greeted by a ranger, and hikes up a steep incline to the prison (proper shoes are a must).

Headsets are distributed for a self-guided audio tour narrated by former inmates and guards. For the full effect of the incarceration experience, the tour leads you into a solitary confinement cell, plays an enactment of a prison uprising, and discusses notorious inmates, including Al Capone, George 'Machine Gun' Kelly and Robert Stroud, the 'Birdman of Alcatraz.'

Night visitors gain access to areas not seen on the crowded daytime tours, including a peek inside the prison hospital. The tour also includes 'extras': special presentations on topics from escape attempts to challenges faced by families who lived on Alcatraz. And the nighttime views of San Francisco are spectacular.

Book early; tours often sell out. Discounts are given for online bookings. Dress warmly and be advised that there are no food concessions on the island, though snacks are available on the ferries.

Alcatraz Night Tour; tel: 888-814-2305; www.alcatraztickets.com; Thur–Mon; Hornblower ferries depart from Pier 33 on Fisherman's Wharf, call for schedule; charge; map G4

Sip **Irish coffee** at an iconic cafe, then jump on a **cable car**

At one time, cable cars traversed the entire city, stretching all the way to the ocean. Three lines remain in existence now – Powell/Mason, Powell/Hyde, and California Street.

For the quintessential experience, board the **Powell/Hyde line** at the Hyde Street turnaround. Beat long cable-car lines by rising early for breakfast at the classic **Buena Vista**, across from the turnaround. This former waterfront saloon still retains its folksy charm and is renowned for mastering Irish coffee, introduced to the United States in 1952. These elixirs, made with whiskey, coffee, and sugar, are topped with a thick layer of chilled cream. Glass mugs line the bar, waiting to be filled.

Climb aboard the car and hang on tightly to the outside rungs. Feel the wind in your face and listen to the clanging bells and the grinding brakes as the little car creaks and groans up the dramatic Hyde Street hill. Turn and look back toward the bay. Even in fog, the views get more breathtaking with each block.

A fascinating stop along the way is the **Cable Car Museum**. Learn about the cars' history, and view massive working engines and the below-street-level cables in the powerhouse.

If rising early to beat the crowds doesn't suit you, the **California Street line**, from Market to Van Ness, is less traveled and passes by the swanky hotels on top of Nob Hill.

Powell/Hyde line; daily 6am–12.30am; map B4
Buena Vista; 2765 Hyde Street; tel: 415-474-5044; Mon–Fri 9am–2am, Sat–Sun 8am–2am; map C4
Cable Car Museum; 1201 Mason Street; tel: 415-474-1887; www.cablecarmuseum. org; daily 10am–5pm; free; map E1

27

Venture aboard **historic sea vessels** at the **Hyde Street Pier**

A collection of vintage vessels, including a graciously appointed houseboat once used as a summer retreat, and a 1914 paddlewheel tugboat, is moored at the Hyde Street Pier.

But the *Balclutha*, an 1886 three-masted sailing ship, steals the show. At 301ft long with a main mast that towers 145ft high, she carried goods around Cape Horn 17 times and had her Hollywood debut in the film *Mutiny on the Bounty*, which was followed by a career posing as a pirate ship. Today, you can explore the ship's vast interior, poke around the captain's quarters, peek into pantries, and watch a video chronicling her long and colorful history that began in the shipyards near Glasgow, Scotland.

For a portal into maritime history, use your cell phone to dial up short, informative audio tours on such topics as dangers at sea, sailors and music, or the Streamline Moderne Deco buildings that can be viewed from the pier. Beware of steep roaming charges if you have a UK phone.

Art Deco fans shouldn't miss the **Aquatic Park Bathhouse Building** (in the Maritime Museum, Beach Street at Polk Street, tel: 415-561-7170), a true gem with dazzling, newly restored murals that were hidden for 50 years.

The fleet is part of the Maritime National Historical Park; 2905 Hyde Street; tel: 415-447-5000; www.nps.gov/safr; daily 9.30am–5pm; charge; map B5

SEA SHANTY SATURDAYS
Warm up your pipes for a unique experience at the free monthly sea shanty sing-a-longs aboard the *Balclutha*, held on the first Saturday of the month (unless the Saturday falls on a holiday) from 8pm to midnight. Reservations are required, and can be made by calling 415-561-7171 or emailing peter_kasin@nps.gov.

Swim in the bay at a century-old rowing club, then **taste perfection** at Gary Danko

In an area that many equate with cheap trinkets and bad street art, two rowing clubs are bastions of authenticity that have endured for nearly 150 years.

For a refreshing glimpse into the soul of the waterfront and an invigorating workout, the **South End Rowing Club** is a place where you can chat with salty locals and take a refreshing dip in the bay. Located next to the Hyde Street Pier in an unassuming clapboard building with a multi-million-dollar view, the humble South End was founded in 1873, making it one of the oldest athletic clubs in the western United States.

Next door, the slightly fancier **Dolphin Club** (*pictured*) maintains a fierce yet friendly rivalry with

its neighbor, and the two compete in an annual triathlon (rowing, swimming, and running).

Though 'membership only,' both clubs are open to the public three days a week for a minimal fee. Boats are reserved for members, but visitors can swim (don't forget the wetsuit!), lift weights, or play handball.

You will want to get in a good workout in preparation for the epic meal that follows. **Gary Danko** is the *ne plus ultra* of San Francisco cuisine – with prices to match. The tasting menu allows you to customize your meal: choose from appetizers like lobster salad with avocado and shaved fennel in a Meyer lemon tarragon vinaigrette, and entrees like filet of beef with curried cauliflower, cumin-cilantro butter and tamarind glaze. The service is as impeccable as the food.

South End Rowing Club; 500 Jefferson Street; tel: 415-776-7372 or 415-929-9656; www.south-end.org
Dolphin Club; 502 Jefferson Street; tel: 415-441-9329; www.dolphinclub.org; the clubs open alternate days Tue–Sat 10am–6pm; charge; map B4/C4
Gary Danko; 800 North Point Street; tel: 415-749-2060; www.garydanko.com; nightly D; map C4

Camp out overnight at **Angel Island**, the Ellis Island of the West

Watch the city recede as you drift across the bay to the romantic, historic, and breathtakingly scenic **Angel Island**.

It is known as the 'Ellis Island of the West,' and some 1 million immigrants – Chinese, Russian, Indian, Japanese, Korean, and others – were detained here between 1910 and 1940 in poor conditions. This dark but fascinating specter of the island's history is chronicled at the **Angel Island Immigration Station** (tel: 415-435-3392; http://aiisf.org; daily 8am–sunset; charge). See re-creations of cramped dorms and read desperate poetry scrawled on the walls by the detainees.

If you plan ahead, you can score one of just nine campsites (nos. 4, 5, and 6 have panoramic views of the city's skyline) and pitch your tent among native bay, oak, and madrone trees. Not a planner? A day trip is still a rewarding escape.

Island recreation includes hiking, biking, fishing and boating. For a relaxing stroll, the 5-mile Perimeter Road circles the island. If you are in the mood for a challenge, tackle the Sunset and Northridge trails to the summit of Mount Livermore: on a clear day, you can see all five Bay Area bridges from the top. Bike rentals and guided Segway tours are other options to tour the island.

Wind down with oysters and Chardonnay at sunset at the **Cove Café** (tel: 415-435-3392). On Saturday (in season), enjoy live music on the Cantina Deck.

Angel Island; tel: 415-897-0715; http://angelisland.org; Blue & Gold Fleet ferries depart from Pier 41 on Fisherman's Wharf, call for schedule; map E5

Frolic with the family at **Fisherman's Wharf**

Let's face it, kids love Fisherman's Wharf. Without subjecting your children to total over-stimulation or another souvenir-and-T-shirt shop, you can too.

For a low-tech good time, the **Musee Mechanique** has more than 300 mechanically operated musical instruments and antique penny-arcade machines. Parents will dig the vintage vibe, and kids will either delight or cry at Laffing Sal, a towering funhouse refugee with a missing tooth that laughs maniacally when the coin drops.

Close by is another children's crowd-pleaser that is also a hit with parents. The **USS Pampanito** is a restored World War II fleet submarine-turned-museum. On the tour you can poke around the cramped interior, check out the engine room and touch the torpedo launcher. The audio tour only costs a bit extra and is well worth it.

Over on Pier 39, kids of all ages are fascinated by sharks and other marine life displayed at the **Aquarium of the Bay** (pictured). Moving walkways through clear tunnels give you a diver's-eye view of the Bay.

When you get hungry, stop for a loaf of crusty San Francisco sourdough at **Bistro Boudin** (160 Jefferson Street; tel: 415-351-5561; map D4), the bakery that debuted the prized bread. A 30ft observation window lets kids (and you) watch the baking in action.

Musee Mechanique; Pier 45; tel: 415-346-2000; Mon–Fri 10am-7pm, Sat–Sun 10am-8pm; free; map D5
USS Pampanito; Pier 45; tel: 415-775-1943; daily from 9am, call for closing time; charge; map D5
Aquarium of the Bay; Pier 39; tel: 415-623-5300; summer daily 9am-8pm, winter Mon–Thur 10am-6pm, Fri–Sun 10am-7pm; map E5

While away a lazy afternoon in **Washington Square**, the heart of North Beach

The undisputed center of North Beach is **Washington Square**. This small green oasis, bounded by Columbus Avenue and Filbert, Stockton, and Union streets, is a natural nexus and gathering place for the surrounding community.

The square is a microcosm of the neighborhood. Anchoring one side is the church of **SS Peter and Paul** (666 Filbert Street; www.stspeterpaul.san-francisco.ca.us), a Neo-Gothic beauty with elegant white spires that pierce the sky. On one corner, a group of

Tai Chi practitioners make slow movements in sync, while on the benches along tree-lined Union Street old men argue in Italian. Dogs chase Frisbees, young women sunbathe, and there is no shortage of strollers circling the park.

Sidewalk cafes and restaurants line two sides of the perimeter, including quirky **Mario's Bohemian Cigar Store** (566 Columbus Avenue; tel: 415-362-0536; daily L and D), an institution on the southwest corner. Sit at an outdoor table, order a cold beer, a glass of wine or an espresso, and a superb panini made from focaccia baked fresh at **Liguria Bakery** (p.34) across the park. You won't be disappointed, unless you were expecting doting service.

One of the few North Beach lodging options is right here in the thick of it. The charming a **Washington Square Inn** (p.178) is the perfect spot from which to appreciate this urban treasure.

Every June, Washington Square is the setting of the rowdy **North Beach Festival**, where revelers assemble to see live music, eat skewered meats, and party.

Washington Square Park; map C2

Linger over a **perfect cappuccino** at one of the city's **great cafes**

San Francisco takes coffee seriously. Look around in almost any neighborhood and you'll see someone rushing by with a 'to go' cup. In recent years Starbucks has been edged out slightly by a new crop of roasteries like Blue Bottle and Ritual Roasters that inspire cult-like followings. Peet's, which began in Berkeley, still thrives. But for a true cafe experience, North Beach offers stylish places to savor your cup, each with its own niche and first-rate people-watching. Relax and sip a beverage as the 30 Stockton bus whizzes by and Chinese grandmothers call out to children.

Caffe Trieste was a favorite haunt of the Beat Generation in the 1950s and is still run by the Giotta family. They roast their beans next door and host a popular, free (with purchase) Italian folk music and opera concert every Saturday.

On a lively strip of Columbus Avenue are **Caffe Greco** and **Caffe Puccini**. You can't go wrong sipping Illy coffee at a sidewalk table at Greco or listening to arias on the jukebox at Puccini and nursing an espresso. Meanwhile, **Caffe Roma** promises coffee as 'black as night, strong as sin, sweet as love, hot as hell.' Believe them.

Caffe Trieste; 601 Vallejo Street; tel: 415-392-6739; Sun–Thur 6.30am–11pm, Fri–Sat 6.30am–midnight; map D1
Caffe Greco; 423 Columbus Avenue; tel: 415-397-6261; Sun–Thur 7am–11pm, Fri–Sat 7am–midnight; map D1
Caffe Puccini; 411 Columbus Avenue; tel: 415-989-7033; daily 6am–midnight; map D1
Caffe Roma; 526 Columbus Avenue; tel: 415-296-7942; daily 6am–7pm; map C1

Get a **bird's-eye view** from the top of **Coit Tower**, then hunt for a hidden tiger below

One of the best urban hikes in San Francisco starts with provisions from **Liguria Bakery** (1700 Stockton Street; tel: 415-421-3786; Mon–Fri 8am–1pm, Sat–Sun 7am–noon), a tiny, century-old Italian bakery in North Beach. Choose a slab of mouthwatering focaccia (they bake nothing else), which is sliced then wrapped in butcher paper and tied with twine.

Start here from the northeast corner of **Washington Square Park** (*p.32*), heading straight up Filbert Street to **Coit Tower**, the fluted white column atop Telegraph Hill, one of the city's most recognized and beloved landmarks. Legend persists that the 210ft Art Deco cylinder was built to resemble a fire-hose nozzle. Take in the sweeping vistas from the foot of the tower or ascend to the top for the ultimate 360-degree view. Stop and admire the vivid, colorful murals in the

lobby painted in the Social Realism style during the Great Depression of the early 1930s.

From Coit Tower, walk back to where **Filbert Street** plunges down the eastern slope of Telegraph Hill and turns into a rambling stairway. The Filbert Steps descend through gardens lush with fuchsia, fennel, lemon trees, bougainvillea, and giant aloe. Charming wooden cottages built into the hill, some by 19th-century sea captains, line the paths.

Pause at the apartment building at **1360 Montgomery Street** (map G3) and gaze at the bas-relief exterior on this Deco masterpiece that depicts the Golden Gate International Exposition of 1939–40. This stunning building was once the setting of lavish parties for the moneyed social set, and was featured in *Dark*

Passage, starring Humphrey Bogart and Lauren Bacall. Before continuing down to Sansome Street, take in the exquisite views, then stroll down Darrell Place and Napier Lane, two tiny, tucked-away streets lined with quirky cottages and verdant gardens.

Once you reach Sansome, lounge by the fountain at **Levi's Plaza**, home to the headquarters of Levi Strauss, the jeans company that started here in 1853.

When you are ready for the most strenuous part of the walk, the **Greenwich Street Steps** (map G3) one block north of Filbert are equally beautiful and slightly less traveled. As you ascend, be on the lookout for quirky mosaic sculptures tucked away in the wild, overgrown gardens. About halfway up, look for a bench partially obscured by foliage and accessed by a dirt path. From the bench, look up the hill through the dense shrubbery for a large reclining tiger, covered in colorful mosaics, concealed from the steps.

Continue climbing past **Julius Castle**, a former restaurant that is now shuttered. The building is still a marvel though; a little castle clinging to the side of Telegraph Hill. The steps wend back up and finish at the base of Coit Tower.

Coit Tower; 1 Telegraph Hill Boulevard; tel: 415-362-0808; daily 10am–5pm; charge; map F3

WILD PARROTS

If you hear loud screeching and chattering from above, look up in the trees – you may have encountered the wild flock of some 200 cherry-headed conure parakeets, descended from a group of domesticated escapees, who forage here for fruit, berries, and nuts. The birds migrate around the area but are often in the fruit trees along the Filbert Steps. A 2005 documentary called *The Wild Parrots of Telegraph Hill* chronicles their sweet, fascinating story.

Indulge yourself with **one-of-a-kind finds** on **Grant Avenue**

The oldest street in San Francisco retains a bohemian flair, but cute boutiques have taken the place of the smoky jazz clubs that preceded them. Hit the shops and explore the neighborhood that gave birth to cool.

Lovers of denim will find their spiritual home at **AB Fits** (no. 1519; tel: 415-982-5726), where impeccable personal service is provided to clothe customers in an assortment of jeans. Trust them, your butt will look good in those.

Ooma (*pictured;* no. 1422; tel: 415-627-6923) is a girly-girl paradise. Colorful racks of flirty dresses, funky shoes, and must-have accessories fill this eclectic, reasonably priced boutique.

For timeless, high-quality women's fashion that flatters, try **Paparazzi** (no. 1424; tel: 415-399-1117). Browse **Lola of North Beach** (no. 1415; tel: 415-781-1817) for smart, small gifts like onesies for babies with irreverent sayings, moleskin notebooks, travel candles, and pastel-colored pens.

South of Grant on Columbus, tiny **Abitare** (no. 522; tel: 415-392-5800) is a true gem selling a well-chosen array of gifts – from luxurious bath products to an assortment of hats and purses to fun stuff for children.

The selection is discriminating, artistic, and seasonal.

For vibrant, distinctive pottery, also on Columbus is **Biordi Art Imports** (no. 412; tel: 415-392-8096). It has a museum-like feel, culling an impressive collection of ceramic art from all over Italy.

After crossing Columbus, Grant abruptly becomes bustling Chinatown, where you will find an abundance of shops that cater to the tourist trade (*p.50*).

Grant Avenue; map D1/D2
Columbus Avenue; map C1/D1

Discover hidden **Jack Early Park**, with a **breathtaking view** of the bay

Don't blink or you will miss the entrance to **Jack Early Park** on Grant Avenue, north of Chestnut Street near Pfeiffer Street. Salvaged wood steps zigzag up from an iron gate on an unassumingly residential block and lead to a cozy bench with a vintage lamppost behind.

Once you find it, savor a hushed, secluded moment away from it all at this postage-stamp-sized park that is essentially not much more that a tiny patch of green clinging to the side of a rocky slope. You might feel like you stumbled upon a secret hiding place that you want to keep to yourself, but this is a sweet spot best shared. Inhale the salty sea air as you gaze upon one of the city's best yet least known views – a slice of the northern waterfront spanning from the **Bay Bridge** *(p.90)* to the **Golden Gate** *(p.156)*.

A platform with a railing is good for leaning on as you take in the surrounding beauty. With the mourn of foghorn in the distance, a passing sailboat in the bay and sunset if you timed it well, you pretty much have the ideal San Francisco moment.

Prolong the mood with an intimate, slow-paced dinner of both savory and sweet soufflés at **Café Jaqueline** (1454 Grant Avenue; tel: 415-981-5585; D Wed–Sun) a few blocks away.

Jack Early Park; map F3

Chuckle over **stand-up comedy** or over-the-top dinner-theater **cabaret**

San Francisco has long held the reputation for being a comedy mecca; and the tradition of irreverent and political humor is alive and well in and around North Beach, with stand-up clubs and outrageous cabaret.

A visit to the legendary **Purple Onion** (140 Columbus Avenue; tel: 415-956-1653; map G1) is a must. The venue has a sophisticated, jazz-club feel, and its stage showcased Lenny Bruce, Woody Allen, and Richard Pryor. Shows are high-quality, but sporadic. Dining at Caffe Macaroni upstairs allows you to reserve a table at the club.

For something more extravagant, book well in advance for the grande dame of SF's stages, **Beach Blanket Babylon** (678 Green Street; tel: 415-421-4222; map C1). Shows here are filled with an array of pop culture icons affectionately skewered with kooky dance numbers and over-the-top haberdashery.

Teatro ZinZanni (Pier 29 on the Embarcadero; tel: 415-438-2668; map G3) dazzles its five-course diners with a carnival of musicians, clowns and derring-doers in an antique European tent *(pictured)*.

You can see the biggest comics from television, like the stars of *Saturday Night Live*, in person at **Cobb's Comedy Club** (915 Columbus Avenue; tel: 415-928-4320; map D3). Arrive at least half an hour before show time to avoid being seated in the balcony.

Nearby in the Financial District, the **Punch Line** (444 Battery Street; tel: 415-397-7573; map p.62 F5) boasts the top club headliners in the country – renowned comic Dave Chappelle often does 'surprise' shows here.

Feast on **authentic Italian food** in San Francisco's 'Little Italy'

A wide assortment of regional Italian flavors converge deliciously in North Beach. Columbus Avenue, the main drag that slices diagonally through the neighborhood, is dotted with tasty trattorias, many offering outdoor seating. You can get a good meal for a fair price at most, but there are a few standout favorites that have weathered the test of time.

The dining room at **Tommaso's** is a few steps below street level. Celebrities and average Joes alike count this warm, inviting family-run restaurant as their own. House specialties include the oven-baked clams and lasagna.

For a taste of local color and Italian comfort food, cram into bustling **Sodini's**. The bar is often peppered with friendly locals. Classic pasta dishes are big enough to split, and service is uber-friendly. **Da Flora** has a sexy, sumptuous vibe and a seasonally inspired menu offering Venetian food with a Hungarian twist.

New kid on the block **Tony's Napoletana Pizza** became an instant neighborhood sensation when it was opened by 'world pizza champion' Tony Gemignani. They also serve a full dinner menu.

Tommaso's; 1042 Kearny Street; tel: 415-398-9696; Tue–Sun D; map G2
Sodini's; 510 Green Street; tel: 415-291-0499; daily D; map D1
Da Flora; 701 Columbus Avenue; tel: 415-981-4664; Tue–Sat D; map E2
Tony's Napoletana Pizza; 1570 Stockton Street; tel: 415-835-9888; Wed–Sun L & D; map C2

Raise a glass to the Beat Generation and thumb through a rare edition of *Howl*

North Beach is one of the geographic epicenters associated with the Beat Generation, an iconoclastic group of writers and free thinkers who made their mark on the American literary scene in the 1950s, challenging the establishment and documenting it in prose and poetry.

If the ghosts of the Beats can be felt in the shadows and dusty corners of North Beach, their presence is perhaps strongest at **Vesuvio**. Legend has it that Neal Cassady stopped here on his way to a poetry reading at the legendary Six Gallery (formerly at Union and Fillmore streets, now closed) in 1955, and later introduced the narrow, cluttered wood-lined bar to his pal Jack Kerouac. The rest can be filed under Beatnik drinking history.

Today, Vesuvio is ground zero for anyone looking to walk in the tattered shoes of the Beats. So go ahead, look around at the memorabilia on the crowded walls, soak in the bohemian spirit, and throw one back for the tortured poets and writers of this restless period in American literature. The alley that runs alongside the bar has been renamed in Kerouac's honor, and Vesuvio sometimes hosts art events there.

> **LITERARY LANDMARK**
> Kerouac is rumored to have written *On the Road* in an amphetamine-fueled three weeks while he resided at the modest home of Neal Cassady and his wife Carolyn (who became Jack's lover) at **29 Russell Street**, (map p.44 A3) near the intersection of Union and Hyde streets on Russian Hill. Stand out front, listen to the clang of the cable cars and imagine Kerouac frantically pecking out his work on a 120ft taped-together scroll.

From here, Beat aficionados can go next door to **City Lights Booksellers & Publishers**, the first paperback bookshop in the United States and one of the great independent sellers, co-founded by Lawrence Ferlinghetti. City Lights published Beat poet Allen Ginsberg's controversial volume *Howl and Other Poems* in 1956, sparking an obscenity trial. Ferlinghetti was acquitted a year later. While he never considered himself a 'Beatnik,' since he was a married war veteran from an earlier generation, he was immortalized as Lorenzo Monsanto in Kerouac's autobiographical novel *Big Sur*.

City Lights attracts visitors from all over the world to browse the stacks of world literature, the arts, and progressive politics. Still a relevant force in the literary community, the bookstore hosts weekly events and author readings.

Around the corner on Broadway near Romolo Alley is the **Beat Museum**. Perusing tidbits and ephemera from the Beats – license plates, letters, signed photos, and the pièce de résistance, the banned edition of Ginsberg's *Howl*, a trophy to free speech – is like a road trip back to the early 1950s without the booze and Benzedrine. On the second floor are shrines to individual Beat artists with artifacts, first-edition books and commemorations. Downstairs you'll find obscure Beat titles, poetry, and local anthologies.

True Beat enthusiasts will want to book a room at **Hotel Bohème** *(p.177)*, where they can absorb even more Beat ephemera and black-and-white photos of the era.

Vesuvio; 255 Columbus Avenue; tel: 415-362-3370; www.vesuvio.com; daily 6am–2am; map F1
City Lights Booksellers & Publishers; 261 Columbus Avenue; tel: 415-362-8193; www.citylights.com; daily 10am–midnight; map F1
Beat Museum; 540 Broadway; tel: 415-399-9626; www.thebeatmuseum. org; daily 10am–7pm; charge; map F2

CITY LIGHTS

Chinatown, Russian Hill, and Nob Hill

Chinatown, Russian Hill and Nob Hill

Take a **temple tour** and go **'dim hopping'**

The places of worship and small dim sum bakeries where the local Chinese pray and shop offer a glimpse into this fascinating community beyond the crowded sidewalks of Chinatown.

Start your tour at the **Tin How Temple** (125 Waverly Place; tel: 415-986-2520; daily 10am–4pm; map D7), where incense strongly permeates the air. Enter through an inconspicuous doorway and leave offerings of fruit and symbolic money to the Queen of the Heavens and the Goddess of the Seven Seas.

The largest Buddhist congregation in the US can be found at the five-story **Buddha Universal Church** (720 Washington Street; tel: 415-982-6116; call to schedule visits; map E7). The church has a rooftop

garden with a lotus pool, a sacred Bodhi tree, and city views.

Above the post office, the **Kong Chow Temple** (855 Stockton Street; Mon–Sat 9am–4pm; map D8) has lovely intricate wood-carvings, a colorful altar to the deity Kuan Ti, and a view of the Transamerica Pyramid.

Once you have taken care of the deities, it is time to indulge in those doughy delights known as dim sum. Forgo the restaurants that serve cart-style and forage the small bakeries on a 'dim hop.' The 700 block of Jackson Street is dim sum central. Start at the **House of Dim Sum** (no. 735) and **Delicious Dim Sum** (no. 752) across the street, but venture further and taste your way through Chinatown, one dumpling at a time.

Sip heady **cocktails** at Chinatown bars, including a former **opium den**

Chinatown after dark is like stepping into another dimension. The sidewalks roll up – gone are the produce carts, buckets of live frogs, and glazed ducks hanging from nooses. Nobody is around to sell you plastic cable cars, snow globes, or key chains. The narrow streets are desolate, and a sense of mystery hangs in the air well after the lanterns flick on. Most of the population has gone home to a family dinner and an early night.

But for the rest, there is the **Buddha Lounge**. A neon-lit cocktail symbol beckons the weary drinker inside for stiff cocktails while a 5ft-tall Buddha looks on from his altar behind the bar. Sink into one of the red vinyl booths, or if you are feeling confident, perch at the bar and challenge a local to a game of liar's dice (an Incan dice bluffing game). Don't expect luxury or even cleanliness. This is a dive bar with cheap drinks, classic tunes on the jukebox, and engaging bartenders.

Across the street, hipsters, regulars, and spillovers from North Beach bars shuffle through the big red doors into **Li Po**, a dimly lit Chinese cocktail lounge with cluttered walls, a massive hanging lantern, and a golden shrine to Buddha. Named for the famous Chinese poet, it's a favourite haunt of tourists and locals alike. The sweaty basement is a former opium den that now hosts live music, DJ dance parties, and karaoke.

Chinatown bars may not be antiseptic, but you visit them for the atmosphere, not for specialty cocktails and hygiene; and take with you an experience you won't forget in a hurry.

Buddha Lounge; 901 Grant Avenue; tel: 415-362-1792; daily 1pm–2am; map D7
Li Po; 916 Grant Avenue; tel: 415-982-0072; daily 2pm–2am; cash only; map D7

Peek into a tiny **cookie factory** and find your fortune

Behind Chinatown's bustling main drags, a labyrinth of narrow alleyways provide respite from the crowd and a deeper look into the neighborhood.

Explore these back alleys on foot and you'll get a real sense of place – the sound of mahjong tiles clacking in smoky back rooms, the pungent smell of incense and spice, and the sight of women laden with pink cardboard boxes from the local bakeries and butchers.

One of the sweetest aromas rises from Ross Alley, the oldest alley in San Francisco, once infamous for gambling houses, opium dens, and brothels. Follow the smell of vanilla to the **Golden Gate Fortune Cookie Factory**, where cookies are handmade by women the old-fashioned way on a conveyor belt of miniature waffle irons. Visitors are welcome to watch the cookies being made, taste a sample, and purchase a bag.

Next door at No. 32 is the **Barber Shop of Jun Yu**, who has serviced the locks of Frank Sinatra, Clint Eastwood, and (allegedly) The Beatles.

Nearby, the tucked-away **Hang Ah Tea Room** (1 Pagoda Place; tel: 415-982-5686; daily 10am–10pm; map D7) is a good option for reasonably priced dim sum.

Golden Gate Fortune Cookie Factory; 56 Ross Alley; tel: 415-781-3956; daily 8am–6pm; free; map D7

CHINATOWN TREASURE
The **Chinese New Year Treasure Hunt** is a sleuthing adventure played out on the streets of Chinatown, North Beach, and Telegraph Hill on the night of the **Chinese New Year Parade**. Teams have four hours to solve clues leading them to local landmarks, obscure buildings, and relics of the past. Players can come as a team or can join others at the event. Clues test map-reading skills and knowledge of pop culture, current events, science, or literature (tel: 415-664-3900; http://sftreasurehunt.com/hunts/chinese_new_year).

Treat yourself to Happy Hour at a **rooftop garden** restaurant or be thrifty at a **hole-in-the-wall**

For a stellar view of the terracotta rooftops of Chinatown, while enjoying half-priced mai tais and potstickers (crescent-shaped dumplings filled with pork, then steamed and browned), Happy Hour (3–6pm) at the **Empress of China** is a delightful way to spend a late afternoon. The ambience of the rooftop garden restaurant and opulent dining room are worthy of the emperors and empresses of the Han dynasty. Luxuriate in style fit for Chinese royalty and capture a unique view that stretches all the way to the bay.

A far less glamorous, old-school Chinatown experience that is easy on the wallet can be had at **Sam Wo**, a hole-in-the-wall deep in the heart of Chinatown. The entrance leads you through the tiny, cluttered kitchen, where you are immediately assailed by the atmosphere – steamy and cramped, with sounds of clanging pots, and cooks shouting orders in Cantonese. Spicy mouthwatering smells waft by as you climb the narrow staircase to the second- and third-floor dining areas. Food is delivered via an ancient dumbwaiter to the upstairs tables. The menu is pretty traditional – chow fun, chow mein, barbecued pork, beef broccoli, and duck are the popular items, but the real bonuses are the great prices, fast service, large portions, and late closing.

Empress of China; 838 Grant Avenue; tel: 415-434-1345; map D7
Sam Wo; 813 Washington Street; tel: 415-982-0596; daily L & D, Mon–Sat until 3am; cash only; map D7

Shop for kites and kimonos, then pamper sore feet with a reflexology massage

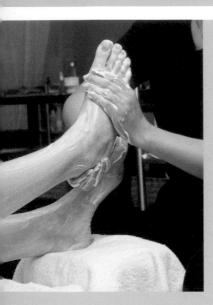

Looking for a bamboo back-scratcher? How about a knock-off Louis Vuitton bag? All the predicable Chinatown kitsch is here on Grant Avenue, but if you're willing to dig a bit deeper among the colorful bazaars, you'll find quality items that you can really treasure.

Hand-embroidered silk kimonos from **China Station** (no. 456) make funky gifts, or can enhance your own wardrobe over skinny jeans or leggings. For guys, silk pajamas are stylish and uber-comfortable.

A few blocks down Grant, foodies flock to **The Wok Shop** (no. 718) for all manner of Asian cooking accessories, from a mortar and pestle to sushi knives to a cast-iron tea set. Home chefs should be prepared to spend some time getting lost in this cook's paradise.

You don't have to be knowledgeable about Chinese medicine to appreciate a stop in one of the old-world herbalists at Washington and Jackson streets. Think of it as a cultural adventure – and don't be surprised to see them calculate your order with an abacus.

When you have had enough of crowds and walking, treat yourself to a reflexology massage at **Lucky Foot Massage** (770 Sacramento Street; tel: 415-399-9698; map E8). Forget pedicures – this attentive treatment, which includes a 10-minute soak and 30-minute massage, takes relaxation to a new level, from the soles up.

Now rejuvenated, it's time to purchase a box kite or windsock from the cramped but charming **Kite Shop** (no. 717) and head off to catch the wind at Ocean Beach (p.131).

Grant Avenue; map D4–D8

Rent a **Mustang convertible** and recreate the scene from *Bullitt*, hugging the **Lombard Street** curves

This famous street, subject of thousands of photographs, snakes its way down three blocks from Hyde Street to Jones Street on Russian Hill. Steve McQueen navigated it expertly in the movie *Bullitt* (give or take the parts shot in different locations in the city, but that's showbiz). For safety's sake, you should take those hairpin turns at half the speed that McQueen did and with twice the caution, or you are likely to take out a camera-toting tourist in your wake.

The meticulously manicured gardens that the twists of **Lombard Street** pass through remain a must-see in this city of phenomenal views. At the bottom, the house at 1000 Lombard is said to be haunted – the assistant of socialite and former *San Francisco Chronicle* columnist Pat Montandon died there in a bizarre accident that remains unsolved.

Two blocks away is the **San Francisco Art Institute**, alma mater of photographer Annie Liebovitz. The handsome terracotta Spanish Colonial building features a cloistered courtyard with a bell tower. A mural called *The Making of a Fresco Showing the Building of a City*, painted by Diego Rivera,

fills an entire wall of the first-floor gallery named for him, and is open to the public.

The laidback cafe (tel: 415-749-4567; call for hours) on campus is a great place to eat breakfast or lunch. They offer seasonal organic food and a magnificent bay view from the sunny open terrace.

Lombard Street; map B2
San Francisco Art Institute; 800 Chestnut Street; tel: 415-771-7020; daily 9am–7.30pm; free; map B2

Don walking shoes and take a tour of the **stairways** of **Russian Hill**

CASTRO STAIRWAYS

If you can't get enough of the secret stairway passages, more are waiting to be discovered across town. Above the Castro neighborhood, between Ord and Levant streets and near 17th Street, are the **Vulcan Street Steps** (map p.134 A4), one of the city's best flights. Detour a half-block from here to find the **Saturn Street Steps** (map p.134 A3). Both pass by tended gardens and homes that can only be accessed from the stairs. Visit www.sisterbetty.org for maps and more information on San Francisco stairways.

Early city planners' haphazard efforts to grid San Francisco's hilly terrain resulted in a walker's dream – more than 350 stairways that connect streets over the hills, some with incredible vantage points.

At 345ft above San Francisco, **Russian Hill**, a magical place of secret gardens and tucked-away cottages, has a concentration of amazing stairway walks.

Writer Armistead Maupin immortalized **Macondray Lane** (*pictured*), a tiny pedestrian street off Leavenworth near Union Street, as Barbary Lane in his *Tales of the City*. In reality, this wooded enclave of overgrown gardens was home to writers and artists before they were outpriced. The rickety wooden steps lead down to Taylor Street.

Parallel to Macondray, the **Vallejo Stairway Garden** starts at the Beaux-Arts-style balustrade at the east end of the 1000 block of Vallejo Street, and zigzags down to Taylor Street, looking east toward the bay.

Nearby, next to 1032 Broadway on top of the Broadway tunnel, is the **Florence Stairway**. Nos. 40 and 42 Florence are examples of Craftsman-style architecture, a reaction to the formality of the Victorian period with a basis in nature, frequently seen among the nooks and crannies of Russian Hill.

Macondray Lane; map B3
Vallejo Stairway Garden; map B3/C3
Florence Stairway; map B4/C4

Barhop at some of the city's swankiest hotels

Nob Hill is the affluent neighborhood where silver barons and railroad tycoons built their lavish mansions high above the city in the late 19th century. Today, it is the location of some of San Francisco's finest luxury hotels.

The first stop on the hop takes you for frou-frou drinks (think coconuts and umbrellas) at the tiki-style **Tonga Room & Hurricane Bar** in the landmark Fairmont hotel (*p.173*). Stay until it 'rains' – a fake thunderstorm heralds the band's arrival.

The party continues across the street with Martinis from the extensive cocktail menu at the sky lounge at the **Top of the Mark** in the Mark Hopkins Hotel. Gaze at an unparalleled 360-degree view of the city, then kick up your heels and dance to live music.

Wind down at the classy piano bar of the **Big Four Restaurant** (*pictured*) in the Huntington Hotel (*p.173*) back across the street on top of Nob Hill. Have a nightcap in front of the cozy fire in a warm, dimly lit men's-club atmosphere.

Tonga Room & Hurricane Bar;
The Fairmont; 950 Mason Street; tel:
415-772-5278; map C5
Top of the Mark; InterContinental Mark Hopkins, 999 California Street; tel: 415-616-6916; map C5
Big Four Restaurant, Huntington Hotel; 1075 California Street; tel: 415-474-5400; map C5

Explore labyrinths and an interfaith chapel at
Grace Cathedral

High on the top of Nob Hill sits lovely **Grace Cathedral**, the Episcopal Diocese of California. Inspired by Notre-Dame in Paris, it was built in the French Gothic style between 1928 and 1964 on land gifted by the family of railroad baron Charles Crocker. The church is a welcoming sanctuary, known for its tolerant views and a policy of inclusion that is refreshing on privileged Nob Hill.

A visit to Grace starts outside the church at the first of its two labyrinths. This one is made of terrazzo stone and the one inside made of sandstone. Walking the paths is a form of meditation – an ancient concept found in many religions and cultures around the world. Take time to walk one and experience the calming effect of this spiritual tradition.

Before you enter the cathedral, stop to marvel at the imposing bronze-and-gold **Doors of Paradise**, replicas cast from the molds of the 15th-century, 16ft-high doors of the Florence Cathedral Baptistery by Lorenzo Ghiberti. The heavy bronze relief depicts scenes from biblical stories.

Walk inside and feel the magnificence of the space. Light filters in through stained glass, dappling the interior in a spectrum of rainbow colors. The leaded glass windows portray diverse concepts – Charles Connick's 23rd Psalm Window above the southern entrance echoes Chartres Cathedral's Jesse Window, while Gabriel Loire's Rose Window above the east entrance depicts St Francis's poem *The Canticle of the Sun*. Look out too for a depiction of astronaut John Glenn, and one that that displays Einstein's $E=mc^2$ formula.

Other treasures within include a 13th-century Catalonian crucifix, a 15th-century French altarpiece, an Aeolian-Skinner organ with 7,466 pipes, a sculpture of St Francis by local artist Beniamino Bufano, and murals portraying the 1906 earthquake and fire that destroyed much of the city.

In the right rear corner, find the **AIDS Interfaith Chapel**. The congregation created it as a memorial to those who have died as a result of AIDS. Here you will see Keith Haring's triptych

altarpiece, *The Life of Christ*, made of bronze and white gold in the style of Russian religious icons. It was Haring's last work, completed two weeks before his death from AIDS in 1990, and embodies his inimitable whimsical style. Another casting of the altarpiece is installed at the Cathedral of St John the Divine in New York City.

You can also see patches from The AIDS Memorial Quilt (www.aidsquilt.org), which was begun in 1987 while the devastating epidemic ravaged San Francisco. Now, more than 91,000 victims' names are on the quilt, pieces of which are displayed across the US.

As you might expect, the Interfaith Chapel includes elements of many world religions, including Christianity, Judaism, Buddhism, Shintoism, and Islam.

Grace has had a men's choir since the church was founded. Rehearsals take place on Sunday mornings at 10.15am and are open to the public. You can also experience the inspirational choir on Thursday evening services at 5.15pm.

Grace Cathedral; 1100 California Street; tel: 415-749-6344; Mon–Fri 7am–6pm, Sat 8am–6pm, Sun 8am–7pm; www.gracecathedral.org; free; map C5

Rejuvenate with a seaweed wrap or guided imagery massage at a **posh spa**

Few towns embrace pleasure like San Francisco. But it's not all fine food and Chardonnay – the *bons vivants* here like to indulge the flesh as well. If you're feeling a little weary and aren't sure you can walk up another hill, book an appointment at the **Nob Hill Spa** and prepare yourself for a superior spa experience fit for a hedonist.

The city's most luxurious spa is located at the top of Nob Hill in the refined Huntington Hotel (*p.173*). Allow yourself plenty of time because you won't want to leave – this is pure, unadulterated bliss.

Once you have checked in and slipped into a comfortable robe, you are free to swim in the infinity pool, relax in the hot tub, sweat out toxins in the steam room and sauna, catch rays on the sundeck, and order food and drinks poolside while enjoying stunning views of the San Francisco skyline.

Services range from traditional massage to body treatments like the seaweed leaf body ritual, which pledges to slim and detoxify. Other choices include a Thai-style massage that includes elements of yoga, the gentleman's facial and a guided imagery massage for deep relaxation.

Little extras are what set the Nob Hill Spa apart. Self-service ginger tea, cucumber water, and fresh fruit are provided. Ice-cold towels are available when you emerge from the steam room and sauna, and a free yoga class is offered with a booked treatment. Caveat: book your service for a weekday and avoid the crowd.

Nob Hill Spa; Huntington Hotel, 1075 California Street; tel: 415-345-2888; www.nobhillspa.com; pool 6am–9pm, services 8am–8.30pm; charge; map C5

Upgrade your home decor on **Polk Street**, then catch a show at **Kimo's**

Polk Street has changed drastically over the years. Gay and transvestite bars have morphed into expensive boutiques and hip restaurants as rents and property values have escalated. Shopping here is eclectic – you'll find a high-end second-hand shop, a Tibetan jewelry store, one of the city's best cheese shops, and a sporting goods emporium all within a block or two.

A side-by-side duet of treasure chests exists at **Molte Cose** and **Bella Cose** (nos. 2036–44), with home adornments, clothing, and accessories artfully strewn around these charming stores. Small still-life oil paintings, desk accessories, barware, and antique glassware mix with lingerie, French soaps, and carefully selected vintage clothing.

Naomi's (no. 1817) has sold one thing for 38 years – American pottery from 1900–50. The shop has been featured by Martha Stewart three times. Tread lightly, though; the owner is a bit cranky.

Also on this block, **One Half** (no. 1837) will jazz up your home on a shoestring. You will find a random collection of rugs, baskets, pillows, candles, and artwork at heavy discounts.

When you are shopped out, grab a bite at **Nick's Crispy Tacos** (1500 Broadway; tel: 415-409-8226; map A4) and venture over to **Kimo's** (1351 Polk Street; tel: 415-885-4535; daily 11am–2am; charge), a Polk Street institution for more than 30 years.

Live music and performance art is featured nearly every night, and if you time it right (Saturday night mid-month) you can witness a time-honored San Francisco tradition – the drag show.

Polk Street; map A4–A6

Slip into a **speakeasy** with a secret **password**

From 1920 to 1933, the sale and consumption of alcohol in the United States was outlawed, and drinking took place secretly in speakeasies. To experience a drink Prohibition-style, time-travel back to the 1920s at **Bourbon & Branch**, an unmarked bar on a seedy block in the Tenderloin. But it is not as easy as just finding it and showing up.

First you will need a reservation and a secret password, which changes daily. Access the bar's website to reserve a table for two hours, then receive a confirmation and the password via email.

Once inside, you must abide by the house rules that include no cell-phone use, no photography, and soft voices. The interior is dark and sexy, with bordello-red wallpaper, antique oak tables, tin ceilings, and intimate booths. In the basement are five secret exit tunnels that allowed for a quick escape from the original speakeasy in the event of a raid. Jazz music plays, and the staff dress in keeping with the retro theme.

The bar menu features plenty of throwbacks as well as creative modern drinks and an extensive collection of bourbons and scotch.

A tip – if you don't have a reservation, ring the buzzer and say 'books.' You will be taken to a secret location where you can enjoy a stiff drink, albeit without seating and from a limited menu.

Bourbon & Branch; 501 Jones Street; tel: 415-346-1735; www.bourbonandbranch. com; Wed–Sat 6pm–2am; map C7

Soothe your soul while grooving to **Gospel music**

For a rousing, rollicking Sunday morning, warm up your pipes and attend a Gospel jam 'celebration' at **Glide Memorial Methodist Church** (known simply as 'Glide'), where uplifting sermons and upbeat music transform a dingy corner of the Tenderloin every week.

A diverse crowd of believers and non-believers, crossing all racial and socioeconomic boundaries, packs a standing-room-only house to listen to the sermons of charismatic San Francisco icon Reverend Cecil Williams and his co-pastor Douglas Finch.

The entire congregation ends up on their feet, swaying shoulders and clapping hands to the beats of the exuberant Glide Ensemble Choir and the Change Band, who passionately belt out Gospel, jazz, and blues. These Sunday services are legendary, with visitors from all corners of the world attending, and are available for sale on CD and DVD. Sharon Stone, Maya Angelou, and Bill Clinton have all been spotted here. Insider tip: arrive 30 minutes early to get a seat.

But Glide is more than a feel-good Christian church. Smack in the middle of one of the city's bleakest neighborhoods, Glide has been assisting the poor and disenfranchised since Williams took the helm in the 1960s. Volunteers serve more than 850,000 meals a year, three times a day, to the hungry.

Glide had its 15 minutes of Hollywood fame with a cameo in the Will Smith movie *The Pursuit of Happyness*, the rags-to-riches true story of a homeless Bay Area man and his son who turned to the church for support.

Glide Memorial Methodist Church; 330 Ellis Street; tel: 415-674-6000; Sun 9am and 11am; www.glide.org; free; map C7

Union Square and Financial District

Union Square and Financial District

| 0 | 100 | 200 | 300 | 400 | 500 yds |
| 0 | 100 | 200 | 300 | 400 | 500 m |

Tin Hou Temple

Kong Chow Temple

Chinese Historical Society of America

California St

Pine St

Bush St

The Ritz-Carlton

Vinto Ct

Pine St

Notre Dame des Victoires

Chinatow Ga

Café de la Pre
Hotel Tr
Harlan

Joan Pl

White Swan Inn

Hotel Rex

Fleur de Lys

Hang Art

Harry Denton's Starlight Room

Campton Pl

Cosmo Pl

Theater on the Square

Sir Francis Drake

Post St

Meyerov Gallery

Cable Car Theater

San Francisco Art Exchange

Stage Door Theater

The Westin St Francis

UNION SQUARE

Xanadu Tribal Arts

Geary St

Hotel Monaco

Curran Theater

ACT Theater

Gold Dust Lounge

Geary St

Macy's

O'Farrell St

O'Farrell St

Antonio St

Stevelov Pl

Hotel Union Square

Ellis St

Ellis St

Great American Music Hall

BOEDDEKER PARK

Exit Theater

Eddy St

Market St

Eddy St

Hotel Metropolis

POWELL ST

Westfield Center

Mus
C

TENDERLOIN

Turk St

Turk St

Golden Gate Theater

The Warfield

Golden Gate Ave

Golden Gate Ave

Islamic Society of San Francisco

Old Mint

McAllister St

CIVIC CENTER PLAZA

Asian Art Museum

Public Library

United Nations Plaza

Orpheum Theater

CIVIC CENTER

62

63

Learn about **Frisco history** while toning your thighs on the **Barbary Coast Trail**

To get acquainted with the history of San Francisco while also squeezing in a picturesque hike, try the **Barbary Coast Trail**, a self-guided walking tour that connects the city's important historic sites.

The mainly flat 4-mile tour begins at the old US Mint (map C1/D1) and weaves north through Union Square (*pictured*), Chinatown, and North Beach, ending in Aquatic Park. The trail is designated by 170 bronze medallions embedded in the sidewalk, and plenty of cafes, bars, and restaurants are along the route should you want to refuel. Both ends of the trail are connected to the Powell/Hyde cable-car line.

Along the trail you will see the birthplace of the Gold Rush, the Pony Express headquarters, a Barbary Coast-era shanghaiing den, sites frequented by the Beats, and the oldest Catholic cathedral west of the Rocky Mountains.

You can order a trail guide by mail or pick one up at local bookstores, but the best way to hit the trail is by downloading the audio tours onto an MP3 player. The sound effects are great – the rumbling of the 1906 earthquake, the Pony Express's clomping hooves, and the unfurling of clipper-ship sails. The three audio tours are nominally priced and can be downloaded from the website. A printable map is included with the tours. For those interested in a guided tour, the tour's creator is available for groups.

Barbary Coast Trail; tel: 415-454-2355; email: info@barbarycoasttrail.org; www. barbarycoasttrail.org; charge

Splurge on **tickets** and enjoy a **night at the theater**

San Francisco's main theater district is concentrated on Geary Street, west of Union Square and in some parts of the Tenderloin neighborhood, where several theaters are all within six blocks of each other.

The three main ones – the **Curran** (445 Geary Street; map C3), the **Golden Gate** (1 Taylor Street; map C1), and the **Orpheum** (1192 Market Street; map A1) – are operated by Shorenstein-Neverlander (tel: 415-551-2000; www.shnsf.com; call for ticket info), who bring original Broadway productions and pre-Broadway premieres to the Bay Area. SHN launched the world premieres of *Wicked, Mamma Mia!,* and *Legally Blonde,* and kicked off the national tours of *Avenue Q, Jersey Boys,* and the revival of *South Pacific.*

ACT (American Conservatory Theater; 405 Geary Street; tel: 415-749-2228; email: tickets@act-sf. org; box office hours noon–6pm on nonperformance days, noon–curtain on performance days; map C3), a theater company and an actor-training conservatory, is based in the Geary Theater. The Tony Award-winning ACT produce a popular rendition of *A Christmas Carol* annually, as well as plays by Bertolt Brecht, David Mamet, Noël Coward, and other greats on the Main Stage.

The independent **Exit Theater** (156 Eddy Street; tel: 415-673-3847; www.theexit.org; map C2) produces the San Francisco Fringe Festival, the largest grass-roots theater festival in the Bay Area, and DIVAfest, dedicated to new works by women writers.

HALF-PRICE TICKETS

Discounted tickets to many of San Francisco's theater productions can be purchased at **TIX Bay Area**, a walk-up box office selling half-price tickets on the day of performance and full-price tickets in advance to select events. The booth is in Union Square on Powell Street between Geary and Post (tel: 415-433-7827; Tue–Fri 11am–6pm, Sat 10am–6pm, Sun 10am–3pm; half-price tickets go on sale at 11am all days).

Get **high above Union Square** in a glass elevator, then drink in the stars

If you find yourself traipsing around Union Square in need of a change of perspective, head to **The Westin St Francis** hotel (*pictured; also p.172*). Cross the lobby to the bank of five glass elevators that cling to the exterior of the Tower Building. Step in and press '31.' Once the elevator clears the hotel building in front, the city panorama unfurls before your eyes.

As you catapult higher, your focus changes from peering into office windows, to staring down on little patches of green rooftop gardens, then to downtown high-rises, the bay and Coit Tower in the distance. This whimsical adventure is not ideal for those who have a fear of heights or popping ears, but it is a cool way to view San Francisco from above.

Another funky glass elevator is at the **Hyatt Regency** at the foot of Market Street. The elevator rises and falls inside a dramatic 17-story atrium lobby, recognized in the Guinness Book of World Records as the largest hotel lobby. It is a great place to wow children and is spectacular during the holidays, when it is strung with cascading strands of twinkling lights.

For those who can't get enough of heights and views but could also use a beverage at this point, **Harry Denton's Starlight Room** is on the 21st floor of the Sir Francis Drake hotel. And while there is no glass elevator here, you can sip a cocktail and drink in the stars.

The Westin St Francis; 335 Powell Street; tel: 415-397-7000; www.westinstfrancis. com; map C3
Hyatt Regency; 5 Embarcadero Center; tel: 415-788-1234; www. sanfranciscoregency.hyatt.com; map G4
Harry Denton's Starlight Room; Sir Francis Drake; 450 Powell Street; tel: 415-395-8595; Tue–Sat 6pm–2am, Sun 11am–3.30pm; charge; map D3

Rock out at The Warfield and gaze at the Baroque-meets-Art Nouveau architecture

For a rocking good time, San Francisco has its share of glamorous concert venues. For the big headlining acts, your best bet is **The Warfield** (*pictured*).

Located a few blocks from Union Square on a seedy strip of Market Street, this marble-and-gilt-swathed palace, rich with Baroque touches like the grand staircase and banisters, sculpted moldings, and glittering brass chandeliers, opened in 1922 featuring vaudeville performers like Al Jolson. It later became a movie theater and in the 1970s it found its calling as a concert venue. Jerry Garcia and the Grateful Dead made it a home base for many years, and everyone from David Bowie and Bob Dylan to The Clash and Gwen Stefani has graced this stage.

Alternatively, nearby in the Tenderloin is the **Great American Music Hall**. A former bordello-turned-jazz club, the space retains the decadent feel of an earlier time – opulent and sumptuous with gilded balconies and heavy Baroque details. It fell into ruin in the 1950s, was saved from the wrecking ball in 1972, and has hosted a variety of performers including Van Morrison, Sarah Vaughan, Gomez, and Galactic.

Across town, on the edge of North Beach, is **Bimbo's**, another nightclub great that still employs hosts to greet guests. Bimbo's has old-world style, and attracts acts like Chris Isaak, The Raconteurs, and Robin Williams.

All offer full bars, dining, dancing, and a truly memorable night on the town.

The Warfield; 982 Market Street; tel: 415-345-0900; http://thewarfieldtheatre.com; map C1
Great American Music Hall; 859 O'Farrell Street; tel: 415-885-0750; www.gamh.com; map A2
Bimbo's; 1025 Columbus Avenue; tel: 415-474-0365; www.bimbos365club.com; map p.24 D3

67

Gallery-hop your way round Union Square

Union Square has a rich commercial art scene. Dozens of galleries are sprinkled throughout the area, with something for everyone's taste – from fine art, photography, and sculpture to contemporary painting and multimedia artwork.

A good place to start a tour of the area is at **49 Geary** (map E3), the location of 20 art galleries, including the popular Fraenkel and Scott Nichols galleries. You could spend hours here wandering through the many galleries, and not even see it all.

Then head one block north to the **Meyerovich Gallery** (251 Post Street; tel: 415-421-7171; map D3), specializing in American and European painting by modern masters like Picasso, Matisse, Hockney, Stella, and Rauschenberg.

Up one block and over a few is relaxed and un-intimidating **Hang Art** (567 Sutter Street; tel: 415-434-4264; map C3),

> **FIRST THURSDAYS**
> At the **First Thursday Night Gallery Strolls** on the first Thursday of each month, many art galleries along Geary, Post, and Sutter streets stay open late and host casual open houses. This is an opportunity to meet local artists, purchase art, drink wine, see and be 'scene,' soak in culture, and peek into galleries that are typically open only by appointment.

who scour the Bay Area for 'fresh art' by exceptional artists. Lastly, stroll back to Geary to see original photographs, paintings, and drawings by and about popular culture artists at the **San Francisco Art Exchange** (458 Geary Street; tel: 415-441-8840; map C3). Rolling Stones guitarist Ronnie Woods's works are sold here.

Party like a prospector at the **Gold Dust Lounge**

The Union Square drinking scene is comprised mainly of hotel bars that tend to be expensive and less relaxed than a typical drinking hole. If you are looking for a laidback place to kick back with a few drinks, there is no need to trek to the Mission, North Beach, or Haight Street when you have the **Gold Dust Lounge**.

Walk toward the Powell/Market cable-car turnaround and look for an old-time theater-style marquee lit all around with small white bulbs above a heavily gilded facade. No, it is not a strip club. A Western-style throwback that was established at the end of Prohibition, the Gold Dust is a neighborhood anachronism. It feels as though it was plucked from another era and dropped into the middle of Union Square.

Inside, worn red velvet banquettes and gilded mirrors line the walls. From the ceiling, ornate chandeliers dangle beneath a fresco of Rubenesque cherubs and Dionysian revelers. The Gold Dust has the faded opulence of a saloon parlor in the Old West. Fortunately, drink prices are retro too.

The crowd is usually a friendly mix of locals and tourists. Happy Hour lasts until 8pm and ushers in young professionals and retail folks for champagne, extra-large margaritas, and Irish coffee, but in general the Gold Dust tends to attract an older crowd.

At night a band is shoehorned into a tiny corner to provide entertainment of upbeat Dixieland jazz, rock, and classics.

Gold Dust Lounge; 247 Powell Street; tel: 415-397-1695; daily 7am–2am; map C3

Shop at a San Francisco institution and see the city's only Frank Lloyd Wright building on **Maiden Lane**

Chic **Maiden Lane** has a checkered past. It was indeed named for the ladies – the type you might meet in a brothel. In the days of the bawdy Barbary Coast, this street was notorious as a rough-and-tumble red-light district with a high murder rate.

Things settled down after the 1906 earthquake and fire ravaged the area. Today, white iron gates close the narrow lane to traffic during the day, when it is dotted with umbrella-shaded tables.

The shopping around here is quite pricey – it is known for bridal couture, designer boutiques, a lavish spa, and, above all, **Gumps** (no. 30), the ultimate San Francisco home decor and gift emporium. Its museum-worthy collection of *objets d'art* – exquisite glass,

bronze figurines, artisan hand-turned wooden bowls, cut crystal, and jade sculptures – is quite a treat. The shop has been a San Francisco institution for 150 years.

Maiden Lane is also notable for architect Frank Lloyd Wright's only building in San Francisco, at no. 140. The Guggenheim-esque V.C. Morris Shop was renovated by Wright in 1948, and is appealing eye candy with graceful curves, a spiral ramp leading to the second floor, circular display windows, and a Romanesque arch. The space is now occupied by **Xanadu Tribal Arts**, a gallery showcasing Asian, Oceanic, and African antiquities. No formal tours are given, but do pop in and look around.

Maiden Lane; map D3/E3

Step back in time at a venerable restaurant

San Francisco is consistently on the cutting edge of cuisine, with chefs embracing new trends and pushing the culinary envelope. This is a wonderful attribute that has resulted in the city being a global gastronomic player, but the flipside is a certain amount of food snobbishness.

At times, there is something both comforting and refreshing about bucking the trends and dining in a venerable restaurant that has been around for more than 100 years.

Tadich Grill is a much-loved institution that has existed in various incarnations since the Gold Rush, with private wooden booths, white linen, waiters in crisp jackets, and the original mahogany bar. The lengthy seafood menu offers every type of preparation imaginable, from lobster Newburg to sand dabs. The cognoscenti order whatever fresh fish is available, grilled.

For steak and Martinis, **Alfred's Steakhouse** supplies an old-school menu and ambience, with dim lights, red leather booths, dark polished wood, and a side of creamed spinach.

Stepping into **Sam's Grill & Seafood Restaurant** is like opening a time capsule into an old-time San Francisco boys' club. Businessmen hunch in curtained booths while gruff waiters in tuxedos serve hearty portions of seafood, steaks, and chops, as well as retro menu items like deviled crab, Shrimp Louie, and sweetbreads.

At all three, you can expect to pay around $45–50 per person for three courses, without wine.

Tadich Grill; 240 California Street; tel: 415-391-1849; Mon–Sat L & D; map F4
Alfred's Steakhouse; 659 Merchant Street; tel: 415-781-7058; Tue–Sat D, Thur L; map E5
Sam's Grill & Seafood Restaurant; 374 Bush Street; tel: 415-421-0594; Mon–Fri L & D; map E4

Parle Français in San Francisco's petite but buzzing French Quarter

A small enclave of French culture is tucked away among the busy streets of San Francisco's Financial District. **Belden Place**, a narrow pedestrian alley, was home to the city's first French settlers, and this street, plus a few surrounding blocks, retain ties to their French culture and ancestry.

Running south from Pine to Bush streets, between Montgomery and Kearny streets, Belden Place is one block long and sits in the shadow of the Bank of America tower. This delightful *rue* is filled with restaurants whose tables spill out into the alley Parisian-style, including the exceptional **Plouf** (no. 40; tel: 415-986-6491; Mon–Fri L & D, Sat D), **Café Bastille** (no. 22; tel: 415-986-5673; Mon–Sat L & D), and **B44** (no. 44; tel: 415-986-6287; Mon–Fri L & D, Sat–Sun D). In addition to French flavors, there are also Italian and Catalan choices, making the street a little slice of Europe in downtown San Francisco.

Nearby are other bastions of French culture, including the lovely **Notre Dame des Victoires Church** (566 Bush Street; map D4), with a mass spoken in French on Sundays at 10.30am.

Two excellent cafes in the French Quarter are **Café de la Presse** (352 Grant Avenue; tel: 415-398-2680; map D3) and **Café Claude** (7 Claude Lane; tel: 415-392-3505; map E3), which hosts live jazz in an intimate setting.

For a special occasion, over in the Tenderloin, romantic, sumptuous **Fleur de Lys** (777 Sutter Street; tel: 415-673-7779; Tue–Sat D; map B3) is one of the city's top French restaurants.

Belden Place; map E4

Feel the ghosts of the **Barbary Coast** while shopping for **antiques and decorative arts**

History oozes from the bricks and cast-iron buildings in genteel **Jackson Square**. Behind the elegant facades, ghosts of the debauched Barbary Coast might still lurk, but this area has evolved into a posh shopping area known for high-end antiques and decorative arts, as well as a sophisticated dining destination. Design showrooms, architectural firms, law offices, and luxury retail have all flocked to this attractive area and made their marks.

Start by browsing the antique dealers: there are nearly 20 within a two-block radius. Most have a specialty – be it 17th-century Continental furniture, 19th-century Californian art, scientific instruments, or antique posters. **Arader Galleries** (432 and 435 Jackson Street) specializes in engravings, lithographs, and paintings; the **Hunt Gallery** (478 Jackson Street) is known for English country antiques and grandfather clocks; while **Argentum – the Leopard's Head** (472 Jackson Street) is devoted entirely to silver.

For a pick-me-up and a history lesson, the **Old Ship Saloon** (298 Pacific Avenue; tel: 415-788-2222; map F5) has a fascinating story, evolving from abandoned Gold

Rush ship to shanghai den to brothel to pub.

Step out of the saloon into this century at **Carrots** (843 Montgomery Street; map E5), a stunning 4,000-sq-ft emporium of carefully curated women's designer clothing, shoes, and accessories, opened in 2007 by sisters who are heirs to a carrot-producing and exporting business.

Finish by going back in time again – to the 1930s at **Bix** (56 Gold Street; tel: 415-433-6300; map E5), a sexy, tucked-away supper club, for cocktails, dinner, and live jazz.

Jackson Square and Jackson Street; map E5/F5

73

Discover **delicious bounty**, then take a stroll along **Herb Caen Way**

The 1989 Loma Prieta earthquake caused its share of devastation, but for San Francisco's **Ferry Building** it was an auspicious occasion, transforming the fortunes of an all-but-forgotten landmark.

Finished in 1898, the handsome structure was crowned with a 245ft clock tower that served as a welcoming beacon to ships on the bay. From the Gold Rush until the 1930s, up to 50,000 people per day passed through the graceful two-story building with its overhead skylights and repeating archways.

The opening of the Bay and Golden Gate bridges in the 1930s changed everything. Autos took the place of ferries, casting the building into obscurity. By the 1950s the Ferry Building was barely used. When the Embarcadero freeway was built, the building was severed from the rest of the city. But two years after the earthquake, the freeway was demolished and plans for development of the Ferry Building Marketplace emerged.

With these plans, the Ferry Building was reborn. Not only has the landmark building been restored to its original grandeur, but it has also become the epicenter of San Francisco's sustainable food movement and an emporium of epicurean delights. A vibrant community of local farmers, artisan producers, and independently owned food businesses exists here, showcasing small regional producers.

The inside **Marketplace** is open daily, with a cornucopia of gourmet treats available to sample and purchase, including local faves **Cowgirl Creamery**, **Acme Bread Company**, **Hog Island Oysters**, and **Recchiuti Chocolates**. There is a teahouse, **Peet's** coffee, a wine bar, independent bookseller **Book Passage** and a high-end kitchen-accessory shop among the many traders. Restaurants anchor three of its corners – **Slanted Door** (tel: 415-861-8032) is definitely worth a splurge for innovative Vietnamese cuisine.

Try to schedule your visit here on one of the days that the **Farmers**

Market descends (tel: 415-291-3276; Tue and Thur 10am–2pm, Sat 8am–2pm). Stands heaped with fresh fruit and veggies, nuts, bread, cheese, jam, flowers, and regional specialty foods spill out of the arcades onto the sidewalk. Saturdays are the big draw – local restaurants set up portable kitchens in the back near the bay, and the area is flooded with foodies of all ilk. It is as social as it is culinary, and has become a Saturday morning tradition for many San Franciscans.

After a morning of indulgence, you might want to burn off a few calories. **Herb Caen Way**, a 3¼ mile stroll from Fisherman's Wharf to the ballpark along the waterfront, is just the antidote.

Ferry Building Marketplace; tel: 415-983-8000; www.ferrybuildingmarketplace.com; Mon–Fri 10am–6pm, Sat 9am–6pm, Sun 11am–5pm; map H5

1:AM **D2**	Four Seasons Hotel **E3**	Red's Java House **H4**
AG Ferrari Foods **E4**	Hosfelt Gallery **E2**	SF Museum of Modern Art **E3**
Asian Art Museum **B2**	Hotel Palomar **D3**	The St Regis Hotel **E3**
AT&T Park (Candlestick Park) **H2**	InterContinental San Francisco **E2**	Tu Lan **C2**
Beard Papa's **E3**	Louise M. Davies Symphony Hall	War Memorial Opera House
Boulevard **G5**	(SF Symphony) **A1**	(SF Ballet) **A2**
Burger Bar **D4**	Macy's **D4**	Westfield Centre **D3**
Burger Joint **G1**	Mel's **D3**	Yerba Buena Gardens **E3**
Cartoon Art Museum **E4**	Metreon **E3**	Yerba Buena Ice Skating and
City Hall **A2**	Momo's **H2**	Bowling Center **E3**
Club 6's On Six Gallery **C2**	Museum of the African Diaspora **E3**	Zeum **E3**
Contemporary Jewish Museum **E3**	Palace Hotel **E4**	
Defenestration **D2**	Phoenix Hotel **B3**	

SoMa and Civic Centre

0   100   200   300   400   500 yds

0   100   200   300   400   500 m

Behold the West Coast's most impressive collection of **20th-century art** at the **San Francisco MOMA**

Designed by Swiss architect Mario Botta, the $65 million **San Francisco Museum of Modern Art** jumpstarted the transformation of the SoMa neighborhood. The building, a blocky brick edifice with a zebra-striped cylindrical turret, courted significant controversy when it came on the scene in 1995. Like much significant art or architecture, people reacted to it – they either loved it or hated it. Still do.

SFMOMA was the first museum on the West Coast devoted to modern and contemporary art. Today it is an anchor in a neighborhood that has evolved from a dodgy low-rent district into a cultural center boasting some six museums within a few blocks.

Enter the museum by stepping into the soaring open atrium, a good meeting spot since you don't present your ticket until you ascend to the galleries above.

The museum's permanent collection contains more than 26,000 works of art across four floors, making it the West Coast's most comprehensive collection of 20th-century art, including painting, sculpture, photography, architecture, design, and media arts. Be sure to see Henri Matisse's seminal *Femme au Chapeau*

(Woman with Hat), painted in 1905. Other painting highlights include Jackson Pollock's *Guardians of the Secret* (1943), René Magritte's 1952 *Les Valeurs Personnelles (Personal Values)*, and works by Paul Klee, Piet Mondrian, Pablo Picasso, Andy Warhol, and Georgia O'Keeffe. Diego Rivera's bold, bright *Cargador de Flores (The Flower Carrier*, 1935) is complemented by Frida Kahlo's *Frida y Diego Rivera* (1931). Also look for Marcel Duchamp's uproar-igniting *Fountain,* his most famous ready-made work. This glazed ceramic urinal is a replica Duchamp created in 1964; the 1917 original was lost. The fine photography collection includes works by Alfred Stieglitz, Edward Weston, Ansel Adams, Dorothea Lange, Robert Frank, and William Klein.

On the second floor look for *Michael,* a rather disturbing life-sized white-and-gold ceramic sculpture of Michael Jackson cradling his pet chimp Bubbles, by pop artist Jeff Koons.

A recent acquisition was the amazing Fisher collection, with 1,100 pieces including works by Cy Twombly, Richard Serra, Roy Lichtenstein, and Willem de Kooning, amongst others.

MOMA MONEY-SAVERS

SFMOMA is closed on Wednesdays but stays open late on Thursdays with half-price admission from 6–8.45pm. On the first Tuesday of each month admission is free. Many museum programs – lectures, films, and curator chats – are included with the ticket price. Also, check out the family offers – kids get in free on the first and third Sunday of the month, and on Family Studios days admission is free for the whole family, with tours and hands-on projects for children (www.sfmoma.org/events).

Beyond the permanent collection, SFMOMA maintains an ongoing schedule of special exhibitions, supplemented by audio guides, educational tours, video screenings, interactive kiosks, and public programs.

The museum has a lovely **Rooftop Garden**, where two open-air spaces and a glass pavilion afford dramatic views of sculptures and the San Francisco skyline. There is also a coffee bar. On the ground floor is **Caffè Museo**, a delightful spot to have a bite. The museum store is on the same floor and well worth a browse.

SFMOMA; 151 Third Street; tel: 415-357-4000; www. sfmoma.org; Thur 11am–8.45pm, Fri– Tue 11am–5.45pm, summer from 10am; charge; map E3

Pirouette across the **ice**, **bowl** a strike or experience **IMAX cinema** at Yerba Buena

At some point you might need a break from museums, galleries, and culture at large. When this happens it is time to go have some fun – and sporty types should check out the **Yerba Buena Ice Skating and Bowling Center**.

The city's only year-round skating center offers public skating, freestyle sessions, discounted family nights, youth skating programs, private instruction, hockey pickup games and a Thursday morning 'Coffee Club' (10am–11.45am), where you warm up with a

coffee, nibble a pastry, then hit the ice for a mini-lesson for $12, including skate rentals. If bowling is more your game, the 12 lanes at Yerba Buena should compel you to roll a few balls.

The Snack Bar, located in the Ice Center, is managed by **Mo's Grill**. You can order beer, wine, soft drinks, and snacks there, but for pizza or more of a meal, Mo's full-service restaurant is directly above the Bowling Center – you can preorder and eat while bowling. It's best to call in advance if you're bringing a large group.

If all that sounds far too strenuous, check out what is playing next door at the **Metreon's** IMAX cinema. IMAX technology can display images of far superior size and quality than traditional film systems. Kick back in the comfy seats and watch a movie on the largest 3D screen in the world.

Yerba Buena Ice Skating and Bowling Center; 750 Folsom Street; tel: 415-820-3532; www.skatebowl.com/ice_center/public/schedule.htm; skating tel: 415-820-3521; hours vary; bowling tel: 415-820-3533; Mon noon–9pm, Tue–Thur noon–10pm, Fri–Sat 10am–midnight, Sun noon–9pm; map E3
Metreon; 101 Fourth Street; tel: 800-326-3264; map E3

Visit an architectural curiosity, the **Contemporary Jewish Museum**, then devour **cream puffs**

The renaissance of the South of Market neighborhood has seen a proliferation of new museums popping up near SFMOMA. One of the newcomers is the **Contemporary Jewish Museum**, which relocated to its striking new building, designed by Daniel Libeskind, in 2008.

On the corner of Mission Street and Yerba Buena Lane, the CJM takes the form of a huge metallic blue steel cube that seems to teeter on the side of the former Jessie Street power substation, in an absurd mashup of contemporary and traditional architecture.

The museum does not house a permanent collection but features traveling exhibitions that explore Jewish culture, history, and art.

After exploring, grab a gigantic cream puff at **Beard Papa's** (99 Yerba Buena Lane; tel: 415-978-9972; map E3) and head to the **Museum of the African Diaspora**, which explores the contributions people of African descent have made across the globe.

Contemporary Jewish Museum; 736 Mission Street; tel: 415-655-7800; www. thecjm.org; Thur 11am–8pm, Fri–Tue 11am–5pm; charge; map E3
Museum of the African Diaspora; 685 Mission Street; tel: 415-358-7200; www.moadsf.org; Wed–Sat 11am–6pm; charge; map E3

Stock up for a **picnic** and then seat yourself for a **lunchtime concert** at Yerba Buena Gardens

The expanse of lush green grass and mature trees at **Yerba Buena Gardens** is the perfect haven in which to escape from the downtown hustle. The 5 acres of meadows, trees, falling water, and public art also make a great picnic location.

First hit **A. G. Ferrari Foods** for the goods. This gourmet Italian food market sells delicious prepared salads and pastas as well as an assortment of meats, cheeses, crackers, and bread. You can also pick up a nice bottle of wine.

Time your picnic to catch a free performance on the esplanade. These take place from May through September, and the diverse bookings range from classical and world music to dance and mime. On Thursday from 12.30–1.30pm is a weekly seasonal lunchtime series. Check the website for other performances.

Then take your time to wander around. On the northeast part of the meadow is a butterfly garden and a woodland grove. The soothing water sculpture on the south side is the **Martin Luther King Jr Memorial and Waterfall**. This inspiring tribute includes backlit photos of the civil-rights movement, shimmering glass panels set in granite, and inscriptions of Dr King's words. Other sculptures are scattered around – look for the whimsical *Shaking Man*. Kids will enjoy the vintage carrousel and rooftop playground.

A.G. Ferrari Foods; 688 Mission Street; tel: 415-344-0644; map E4
Yerba Buena Gardens; bounded by Mission, Folsom, Third, and Fourth streets; tel: 415-820-3550; www.yerba buenagardens.com; daily 6am–10pm; free; map E3

Stimulate young minds at high-tech Zeum or low-tech Cartoon Art Museum

In this culture-vulture neighborhood, it can be hard to sustain the interest of restless kids and teens. Thankfully, two attractions are bound to spark their imaginations.

At **Zeum**, kids drive the experience, blending technology tools with art. Choose to make a music video, compose a soundtrack, create a clay animation, or experiment with digital art. Special workshops allow families to work with artists on topics ranging from robotics to DJ technology. Working in Zeum's production lab, families can play at being a director and bring 3D characters to life. At the end of the day, you will have a cool product to take home. There is also a museum store with innovative, hard-to-find toys.

Maybe your family is up for something a bit more low-tech. Luckily, the **Cartoon Art Museum** is nearby. Browse the collection of 6,000 pieces of original cartoons and animation, which includes editorial cartoons, comic books, Sunday funnies, graphic novels and anime. Past exhibitions have included *The Art of Sleeping Beauty, Gross, Gruesome and Gothic*, and *Rejection Collection: Not in the New Yorker Cartoons*.

A good option for lunch or dinner is **Mel's**, a legendary diner whose original location played a starring role in director George Lucas's first feature, *American Graffiti*. Mel's offers a large menu of standard American diner food – a crowd-pleaser for the shorties.

Zeum; 221 Fourth Street; tel: 415-820-3320; www.zeum.org; Wed–Fri 1–5pm, Sat–Sun 11am–5pm; charge; map E3
Cartoon Art Museum; 655 Mission Street; tel: 415-227-8666; http://cartoon art.org; Tue–Sun 11am–5pm; charge; map E4
Mel's; 801 Mission Street; tel: 415-227-0793; map D3

Consult a **personal shopper** and upgrade your wardrobe at the **Westfield Centre**

There is much good shopping to be done throughout San Francisco, but if you want a glamorous excursion beneath one roof, the **Westfield Centre** is the place to go. In recent years, the centre has been renovated, with the addition of many more shopping and dining choices. The original Art Deco escalators and steel-and-glass dome were restored, and the stylish mall swathed in marble.

With 170 retail options, you will find an array of shops from fine leather goods at **Furla** (Level Two, no. 269), to modern classic menswear at **BOSS Hugo Boss** (Street Level, no. 181), to flirty women's apparel at **bebe** (Level Two, no. 232).

But when it comes to shopping for ourselves, some of us could use a little guidance. That is where the personal shopping experts at **Nordstrom** (Level Four, no. N1; tel: 877-283-4048; http://shop.nordstrom.com) step in. Nordstrom is an upscale department store that occupies the top four floors of the original part of the mall, and is known for impeccable customer service.

One complimentary amenity they offer is the service of a personal stylist. Make an appointment by calling ahead or filling out a form online. The stylist will work within your budget, offer personalized style advice, assist you in putting a look together for a special occasion, and find key pieces to amp up your wardrobe. They are also known for their expert tailoring shop and bra-fitting services.

There are also numerous food outlets, from Pan-Asian **Straits** to Mexican **Zazil**, and a nine-screen cinema, the **Century Theatre**, on the top floor.

Westfield San Francisco Centre; 865 Market Street; tel: 415-512-6776; http:// westfield.com/sanfrancisco; Mon–Sat 10am–8.30pm, Sun 10am–7pm; map D3

See **furniture leaping** from windows and other edgy art on a **SoMa gallery walk**

An edgier, grittier art scene than those elsewhere in the city can be found exploring Sixth Street. You will need to steel yourself against the homelessness in this area – it is not overtly dangerous, but the poverty can be overwhelming. Keep your wits about you as you explore this burgeoning counterculture, reminiscent of New York's Lower East Side.

Start on the corner of Sixth and Howard streets and look up. Here you will see **Defenestration** (www.defenestration.org), a quirky example of public art that was intended to be temporary but captured the collective San Franciscan imagination. Furniture – lamps, armoires, couches, and tables – welded to the outside of the decaying Hugo Hotel appears to be leaping from windows.

Turn right and you will arrive at **1:AM** (First Amendment;

1000 Howard Street; tel: 415-861-5089), a gallery dedicated to street and urban art. Check out their whimsical selection of toys, clothing, and art supplies.

Continue south to **Hosfelt Gallery** (430 Clementina Street; tel: 415-495-5454) to see works by an international roster of emerging and mid-career artists, with a sister gallery in Hells Kitchen, NYC.

Finish the tour back at **Club 6's Onsix Gallery** (60 Sixth Street; tel: 415-863-1221), a club space that hosts a range of artwork from high-end to street, plus live music and DJs. If you've worked up an appetite, reward yourself at **Tu Lan** (8 Sixth Street; tel: 415-626-0927), a cramped, hole-in-the-wall restaurant that serves delicious Vietnamese food. The imperial roll noodle bowl will not disappoint.

Sixth Street; map C2/D2

87

Pay homage to **Harvey Milk** at the **City Hall** rotunda

The first openly gay elected official in the United States, Harvey Milk was voted to the San Francisco Board of Supervisors in 1977. During his 11 years in office he passed a stringent gay-rights ordinance and championed protection for gay citizens.

Milk was a charismatic leader and a brilliant and stirring speaker. He came to be known as the 'Mayor of Castro Street,' but not everyone agreed with his politics and lifestyle. The assassination of Milk and Mayor George Moscone by Dan White, a former police officer and city supervisor who had clashed with

Milk over gay issues, rocked the city on November 27, 1978.

Visit **City Hall** to pay your respects to Harvey Milk and his legacy. A bronze bust of a smiling Milk was unveiled in the rotunda of City Hall in 2008, 30 years after he was gunned down in this same building and the same year his story was brought to the big screen in the acclaimed *Milk*. Thousands of gay marriages were performed here before California's Proposition 8 denied homosexuals the right to marry.

The building itself is worth visiting – a gorgeous example of Beaux-Arts architecture, with a grand marble staircase fanning out beneath the huge graceful dome.

City Hall; 1 Dr Carlton B. Goodlett Place; tel: 415-554-4933; http://sfgsa.org; Mon–Fri 8am–8pm; free; map A2

MILK'S MESSAGE

Harvey Milk made a tape recording on November 18, 1978, with instructions to be read if he died by assassination. With chilling prescience, the recording said, 'If a bullet should enter my brain, let that bullet destroy every closet door.' He was killed nine days later. Upon his death, Milk became an instant martyr for gay rights and a hero to the community.

Seek enlightenment in the presence of the oldest known **Chinese Buddha**

A true gem located in San Francisco's former public library building, the **Asian Art Museum** holds one of the most comprehensive collections of Asian art in the world, spanning 6,000 years of history.

The permanent collection here touches on all the major cultures of Asia, and galleries are divided by geographic regions – South Asia, the Persian World and West Asia, Southeast Asia, the Himalayas and Tibet, China, Korea, and Japan.

One of the most celebrated pieces is a gilt bronze Buddha dated AD 338 – the oldest-known dated Chinese Buddha, and a textbook example of Chinese Buddhist art.

A good tip – if you go to the museum's website before you visit, you can listen to or download podcasts that explain various items in the collection. Free self-guided audio tours are also available at the information desk. Look for the headphone icon in the galleries for items described on the tour.

Free 45-minute expert guided tours are also offered on topics like the treasures of Korea, the kingdoms and cultures of Southeast Asia, or the architecture of the building, a dynamic blend of Beaux-Arts and modern design, and a creative reuse of the former library.

On Sundays at 1pm, the 'storytelling corps' examines selected art objects on display, and gives lively retellings of stories relating to the works.

Stop after at **Café Asia** for fresh sushi, sandwiches, wine, beer, sake, and authentic Asian tea.

Asian Art Museum; 200 Larkin Street; tel: 415-581-3500; www.asianart.org; Tue–Sun 10am–5pm, Thur until 9pm; charge; map B2

Taste **California cuisine**, then feast your eyes on the lights of the **Bay Bridge**

The hallmark of California cuisine is the use of ultra-fresh, seasonal ingredients, produced locally. A temperate climate that enables the state's agricultural abundance, plus the health-conscious lifestyle associated with California, contribute to this culinary movement; organic farming and the array of farmers' markets further underpin the philosophy.

Chef Nancy Oakes is at the helm of **Boulevard**, one of the city's great restaurants and a shining example of California cuisine at its finest. Located in the sumptuously decorated Audiffred building, it pairs a top-notch menu with a romantic Belle Epoque ambience. The Boulevard experience is a truly sensual feast.

The reverence and respect given to the food and its preparation is apparent on the plate, be it a medjool date and arugula salad, or a wood-oven roasted filet mignon. Dessert might be a selection of artisanal cheeses, or éclairs made in small batches to retain a home-baked quality.

After savoring your meal, work off the calories by heading out for a leisurely night stroll. Cross the Embarcadero in front of Boulevard and wander down the length of Pier 14 that juts out into the bay. Silver swivel chairs invite you to relax and take in the breathtaking view of the **Bay Bridge**, with its glittering strands of lights that illuminate the waterfront.

Boulevard; 1 Mission Street; tel: 415-543-6084; www.boulevardrestaurant. com; Mon–Fri L & D, Sat–Sun D; $65 per person, three courses, no wine; map G5

Spend a night of **high culture** at the San Francisco **Ballet or Symphony**

There is no shortage of high culture in San Francisco – the city enjoys a world-class ballet company and symphony, both located in beautiful buildings within two blocks of each other.

Founded in 1933, the **San Francisco Ballet** is the oldest professional ballet company in the United States, and today it is one of the three largest companies in the country.

Director Helgi Tomasson, who took the helm in 1985, has nurtured young talent, commissioned new works, and introduced fresh interpretations of classic ballets. The result is a sophisticated, diverse international repertory.

To make performances more accessible, $20 tickets are available to all ballets. There are also standing-room-only options, and students and teachers pay half-price – so don't forget your ID. Following the ballet on Facebook and Twitter can also net you discounts.

Rising like a phoenix, the **San Francisco Symphony** emerged not long after the 1906 earthquake and revitalized the city's cultural life. In 1985, Michael Tilson Thomas's tenure began, and the symphony has expanded and innovated. They even have their own recording label. Thomas, known here as 'MTT,' initiated the American Festival, as well as others focusing on Stravinsky, Mahler, and Beethoven.

San Francisco Ballet; 301 Van Ness Avenue; tel: 415-86-2000; www.sfballet. org; check website for schedule; map A2 San Francisco Symphony; 201 Van Ness Avenue; tel: 415-864-6000; www. sfsymphony.org; check website for schedule; charge; map A1

Step on the field where the **Giants play baseball** on a **behind-the-scenes tour**

San Francisco's Major League baseball team, the Giants, are steeped in history and beloved by people from all walks of life. In 2000, baseball took a great leap forward with the opening of **AT&T Park**, an architectural delight directly on the waterfront in South Beach's sunny China Basin.

Replacing distant and drafty Candlestick Park, this park features perfect sightlines, fantastic food, a grand view of the Bay Bridge, easy public transit, and its highlight – 'splash hit' home runs into McCovey Cove in the bay over the right-field wall.

The park offers behind-the-scenes public tours, letting you step onto the legendary field and visit the dugouts, batting cages, clubhouse and press box, and a luxury suite.

Game tickets for the visitor are best found online at http://stub hub.com – though for many games tickets are available at the box office on the day, with most seats between $15–85. Locals know you can also watch the game for free from the right-field promenade.

Arrive early to circle the ballpark and see statues of Giants greats Willie Mays, Willie McCovey, and Juan Marichal, and walk the waterfront promenade where boats vie for positions to scoop up home-run balls.

For pre-game festivities, a cluster of sports bars and restaurants have sprung up in the area, the best being the boisterous patio of **Momo's** (760 Second Street; tel: 415-227-8660; map H2).

AT&T Park; 24 Willie Mays Plaza; tel: 415-972-2400; http://sanfrancisco. giants.mlb.com; tours daily 10.30am and 12.30pm excluding game days; charge; map H2

Wash down a **cheeseburger** with a beer at a blue-collar mainstay **on the waterfront**

In a town so heavily influenced by California cuisine and the sustainable/artisan food movement, one might think that a greasy little waterfront burger joint would hardly stand a chance. And while it is pretty clear that they are not serving grass-fed, farm-raised beef, **Red's Java House** is still standing in the shadow of the Bay Bridge, as it has since 1923.

Red's is a place where a broad cross-section of San Franciscans – dockworkers, professionals, hipsters, firefighters, hippies, bikers, construction workers, and baseball fans – can come together in appreciation of a cheap, basic meal. The 'special' is the standard order – a double cheeseburger with fries and a beer that comes to about $7. Other menu items include hotdogs, chili, sandwiches, and spicy Bloody Marys. That Red's is so close to the ballpark where the San Francisco Giants play home games is a boon to fans. Outside tables have extraordinary views, but expect no frills and marginal cleanliness here.

Those who *are* seeking frills are best off heading across town to Macy's, where celebrity chef Hubert Keller helms the **Burger Bar**. Here you can build a burger using such ingredients as Kobe beef, buffalo meat, lobster, salmon, blue cheese, and baby spinach. If money is no object, order the $60 Rossini topped with caramelized onions, shaved truffles, and foie gras.

For middle-of-the-roaders, **Burger Joint** (http://burgerjointsf.com) and **BurgerMeister** (www.burgermeistersf.com) are both solid choices, and each has three locations.

Red's Java House; Pier 30; tel: 415-777-5626; Mon–Fri 7am–5pm, Sat–Sun 9am–5pm; map H4

Burger Bar; sixth floor, Macy's Union Square; tel: 415-296-4272; daily L & D; map D4

Central Neighborhoods

Central Neighborhoods

```
0    100   200   300   400   500 m
0    100   200   300   400   500 yds
```

50 Mallorca **C2**
2044 Jefferson **B2**
2066 Chestnut **C2**
2221 Beach **B2**
2963 Webster **D3**
Absinthe **E7**
Arlequin **E7**
Bar 821 **C7**
Beach Street **B2/C2**
Blue Bottle **E7**
Bulo **E7**
Candybar **C7**
Chateau Tivoli **D7**
Disco **B4**
Erica Tanov **D4**
Exploratorium **B2**
Fillmore Auditorium **D6**
Fisherman's Wharf
  Hostel **D1**
Flood Mansion **D4**
Fly Bar **C7**
French Second Empire **D7**
Gimme Shoes **E7**
'Gold Coast' **B4**
Greens **D1**
Haas-Lilienthal House **D4**
Heidi Says **D4**
Jefferson Street **B2**
Kabuki Springs & Spa **D6**

La Boulangerie **E7**
Lemon Twist **E7**
Lush Life Gallery **D6**
Lyon Street Stairway **B4**
Magic Theatre **D1**
Margaret O'Leary **D4**
Marina Middle School **C2**
Minibar **C7**
Mifune **D5**
Momi Toby's Revolution **E7**
Café and Art Bar **E7**
Museo Italo Americano **D1**
New People **D5**
Nopa **C8**
Octagon House **D3**
Painted Ladies of Alamo
  Square (Seven Sisters)
  D7
Palace of Fine Arts **B2**
Paper Tree **D5**
Peace Plaza **D6**
St John Coltrane African
  Orthodox Church **D6**
SPQR **D5**
Sunhee Moon **D5**
Takara, Ichiban Kan **D6**
Westerfield House **C7**
Yoshi's **D6**

Put **a little magic** in your life at **Fort Mason**

A military base for more than 200 years, the 13-acre waterfront of enchanting, windswept **Fort Mason** once served as an embarkation point for troops and supplies headed to the Pacific during the World War II and the Korean conflict. In 1977, Fort Mason was transformed into a cultural center, and the Mission Revival buildings house nonprofit organizations and host 15,000 different kinds of event each year.

Founded in 1967, the **Magic Theatre** (Building D; tel: 415-441-8822; http://magictheatre.org) is dedicated to the development and production of new plays, and has premiered works by a roster of writers that includes Sam Shepard, David Mamet, and Michael McClure. Since its inception, the Magic Theatre has produced the premieres of more than 200 new works. Tickets range from $15–$55.

During the day, you can visit the **Museo ItaloAmericano** (Building C; tel: 415-673-2200; www.museoitaloamericano. org; Tue–Sun noon–4pm, Mon by appt; free), devoted to Italian and Italian-American art and culture. The permanent collection includes Beniamino Bufano's serene, minimalist marble sculpture *Cat* and Alberto Cristini's bronze *Acrobat*.

For dinner, airy, spacious **Greens** (Building A; tel: 415-771-6222; daily Br, L & D; $50 per person, three courses no wine), in an artsy converted warehouse overlooking the yacht harbor and the Golden Gate Bridge, is a gourmet vegetarian restaurant that will impress even diehard carnivores with its robust, flavorful dishes.

Fort Mason; tel: 441-3400; www. fortmason.org; map D1

Meander through the **Marina**, admiring the wealth of **Art Deco architecture**

The Marina is an affluent neighborhood of pastel houses, restaurants and cafes, chic children's shops, young professionals, and moms pushing baby strollers. You can also find many examples of Art Deco architecture in this sunny bayside enclave.

This lavish design movement, a reaction to the austerity of World War I, lasted from 1925 until the 1940s. People craved whimsy and gravitated toward zigzag patterns, stepped motifs, sunbursts, stylized florals, and exotic Mayan and Egyptian imagery. Following in its footsteps was the Streamline Moderne movement, which took inspiration from speed, motion, and aviation. Nautical images like porthole windows and rounded corners are also part of the style.

Once you know what to look for, it is fun to wander around the Marina looking for Deco design. Flats at 2221–2223 and 2227–2229 **Beach Street** (map B2) are good examples, and 2044–2046 Jefferson (map B2) embodies the nautical look. The Streamline-style flats at 50 Mallorca (map C2) feature incised step lines at the cornice, curved facade bays, and vertical prisms. Look out, too, for the ornate lobbies of apartment buildings, particularly those at 3665 Scott Street.

The **Marina Middle School** (map C2) at 3500 Fillmore Street has many Deco features. The largest building in the Marina district, it is a mixture of Greek Revival and Moderne, decorated with reverse pilasters, decorative roundels with lions, rams, and a bare-breasted maiden.

On **Chestnut Street** (map C2), the building at nos. 2066–2068 features Mayan-style arch windows. At nos. 2124–2130, observe the large silver-painted sunray design on the facade.

If you prefer to embark on a free, organised walking tour, contact City Guides (tel: 415-557-4266; www.sfcityguides.org).

Bend your brain at the **Exploratorium**, an interactive **science museum**

The lovely **Palace of Fine Arts** was designed by Bay Area architect Bernard Maybeck as a temporary structure at the Panama Pacific Exposition of 1915. More than a century and a few restorations later, the romantic, colonnaded building still stands.

Inside the Palace, you will discover the **Exploratorium**, a pioneer of interactive museums and a hangar-sized location for hundreds of fascinating science, art, and human perception exhibits. Founded by physicist and teacher Dr Frank Oppenheimer, the intention here is to spark curiosity about science through hands-on exhibits that you can pick up, tinker with, and touch. The museum's staff have emphasized perception as the means to explore our relationship with light, color, sound and hearing, touch, and heat.

Some 400 exhibits are on display at any given time. Learn about earthquakes at 'Life Along the Faultline,' explore the science behind skateboarding at a sports exhibit, watch a robot sumo-wrestling competition, and discover how your life is affected by nanotechnology in 'Nanomedicine: Tiny Science, Big Questions.'

The **Tactile Dome** is an excursion into total darkness, in an encased geodesic dome where your sense of touch is your only guide. Though clearly not for everyone, it is a popular exhibit.

Outside the Palace, the shimmering swan lake, with an expanse of lawn in front, affords a nice place to picnic and a popular spot for wedding photo shoots.

Exploratorium at the Palace of Fine Arts; 3601 Lyon Street; tel: 415-561-0360, Tactile Dome reservations tel: 415-561-0362; www.exploratorium.edu; Tue–Sun 10am–5pm; charge; map B2

Scale the **Lyon Street steps** and catch a glimpse of **Gold Coast mansions**

Pacific Heights is perhaps the most affluent neighborhood in San Francisco, with extravagant multi-million-dollar mansions built on top of a hill that boast jaw-dropping views of the bay, the Golden Gate Bridge, Alcatraz, and the Marin Headlands.

At 370ft above sea level, the streets of Jackson, Pacific, and Broadway span the most scenic areas along the hill's crest. The section of Broadway stretching from Divisadero to Lyon streets is known as the **'Gold Coast,'** since those who prospered from the Gold Rush built the original mansions. Today this upscale neighborhood is home to the Getty family (billionaire oil company heirs) and

Peter Haus (Levi Strauss heir), as well as rock stars, politicians, and the power elite.

The best way to view the estates, capture the vistas and breathe the rarefied air of the mega-rich is via the **Lyon Street** stairway. Start at Green Street and climb 288 steps past perfectly manicured gardens bursting with blooms, fruit trees, and a terracotta terrace with a fountain. Runners and joggers will likely whizz by on either side: this is a popular workout spot for locals.

Once at the top, the view from Broadway is exquisite. Meander along the magnificent mile of the Gold Coast and peer at the astounding estates. At 2222 Broadway is the palatial **Flood Mansion**, a magnificent Neoclassical Revival building that is now part of the exclusive Schools of the Sacred Heart.

Lyon Street; map B4

Forage for fashions on upper Fillmore Street, then feast on modern Roman cuisine

Upper Fillmore Street is a fashionista paradise: chic local designers have set up shop here, and the street pulses with style. Ramble down the hill, stop by the boutiques, then have a Roman feast at one of the city's most happening restaurants.

Heidi Says (nos. 2416 and 2426) operates two boutiques – look for trendy jeans, T-shirts, and sweaters at 'Casual,' and suits, cocktail dresses, and luxury lines at 'Collections' two doors down. A Heidi Says shoe salon is a few blocks down the hill.

A few steps away, **Erica Tanov** (no. 2408) womenswear, linens, and children's clothing is soft and subtle, with clean lines and careful attention to detail. The collection is made here in San Francisco.

At the corner of Fillmore and Washington, you will find the comfy yet fashionable knits and sportswear of San Francisco-based **Margaret O'Leary** (no. 2400), who uses eco-friendly materials like bamboo yarn and organic cotton to create socially conscious clothing.

A few blocks south at local designer **Sunhee Moon** (no. 1833/101), classic shapes have a splash of edginess that reflects San Francisco style. The looks are versatile and structured in a wide palette of solid colors.

Be sure to have a reservation for dinner at acclaimed **SPQR** (no. 1911; tel: 415-771-7779); you will not be disappointed by the creative interpretation of Roman cuisine.

Upper Fillmore Street; map D4–D6

Bask in **rock 'n' roll history** at the Fillmore Auditorium or **cool jazz** at Yoshi's

No music-lover's trip to San Francisco should be without a visit to the **Fillmore Auditorium**. The incubator of the San Francisco sound in the 1960s, it helped spawn the careers of Janis Joplin, Jefferson Airplane, and the Grateful Dead, and became a nexus for psychedelic music and counterculture.

Promoter Bill Graham launched his empire here, and hosted rock legends like Jimi Hendrix, The Who, Pink Floyd, and The Doors, as well as soul and jazz favorites Aretha Franklin, Otis Redding, and Miles Davis.

The Fillmore continues to hold its own as one of the best and most beloved music venues in the city. Grab an apple as you walk in the door, marvel at the amazing photos, posters, and historical ephemera on the walls, then wait for the lights to go down, leaving the chandeliers bathed in purple light. Upstairs, you can order food from the kitchen catered by renowned chef Wolfgang Puck, and listen to acoustic music between the main acts' sets.

Around the corner in the revitalized jazz district is the stylish and sublime **Yoshi's**. The 28,000-sq-ft, two-story, state-of-the-art venue opened in 2007 and features a roster of local, national, and international jazz talent. Yoshi's also serves mouthwatering Japanese cuisine in an open kitchen inside the magnificent lofty space. An adjoining art space, **Lush Life Gallery**, is part of the Jazz Heritage Center and specializes in jazz-themed art.

The Fillmore; 1805 Geary Boulevard; tel: 415-346-3000; www.thefillmore.com, check website for schedule; map D6
Yoshi's; 1330 Fillmore Street; tel: 415-655-5600; www.yoshis.com; music and dinner nightly; charge; map D6

Unwind in **steam and saunas** or splurge on a shiatsu massage at the **Kabuki Spa**

The traditional Japanese baths at **Kabuki Springs & Spa** are a wonderful way to relax, rejuvenate, and detoxify the body and spirit.

Enter into this peaceful, aromatic sanctuary in Japantown, and pour yourself a cup of sweet tea. Soft new-agey music plays in the background, Buddha statues peek out from niches, and guests speak in hushed tones. You will be handed a robe at the front desk and shown to the lounge if you are opting for a masterful, restorative shiatsu massage.

If you are going straight to the communal baths, stow your clothes in a locker and enter the expansive, sparklingly clean bathing area with muted lighting, Japanese seated baths, Western-style showers, a hot pool, cold plunge, sauna, and steam room. Help yourself to chilled lemon water, complimentary bath products and body-polishing sea salts, and commence bathing.

It is recommended that you wash and rinse before using the pools. For a blissful cleanse, begin with the dry sauna or steam room. Follow with a plunge into the invigorating cold pool to stimulate circulation. A resting period is advised before entering the hot pool. This large pool is kept at 104 degrees and is the last stage in this relaxing ritual.

The baths are clothing-optional and open to women only three days a week (Sundays, Wednesdays, and Fridays) and men only the alternate days (Mondays, Thursdays, and Saturdays). Tuesdays are co-ed, and bathing suits are required.

Kabuki Springs & Spa; 1750 Geary Boulevard; tel: 415-922-6000; www. kabukisprings.com; daily 10am–9.45pm; map D6

Savor **sushi and sake** at one of many Japantown restaurants, then **glimpse the future** at New People

The bulk of **Japantown** is comprised of three long blocks of indoor malls in a commercial district anchored by the **Peace Pagoda.** It has the look and feel of a place that has languished since the 1970s, though the pedestrian-only corridor lined with cherry trees on Buchanan Street is more aesthetically pleasing and the area is filled with interesting shops and restaurants.

Roam around and stop at one of many home-style Japanese restaurants, like **Takara** (22 Peace Plaza, no. 202) or **Mifune** (1737 Post Street), where you can slurp bowls of soba noodles, savor rolls of maki and fresh pieces of sashimi, and sip sake inexpensively.

Shopping is fun here, too. At **Ichiban Kan** (22 Peace Plaza, no. 540) everything – from homewares to imported snack foods to bath products – costs little more than $1. Japanese paper-craft merchant **Paper Tree** (1743 Buchanan Street) has a wealth of books and supplies and a gallery of intricate, beautiful origami pieces.

Catapulting Japantown into this millennium with J-Pop style and energy is **New People** (1746 Post Street; www.newpeopleworld. com). In an ultramodern glass building are an art gallery, an anime cinema, edgy retail, and the Store, where you can pick up cool papers, manga, or even a robot.

The entire area swarms with taiko drummers, martial arts demonstrations, and Japanese street food during the two big annual events – the **Cherry Blossom Festival** in April and the **Nihonmachi Street Fair** in August.

Japantown; map D5/D6

Praise the Lord **jazz-style** at **St John Coltrane** African Orthodox Church

American tenor saxophonist John Coltrane inspired his share of believers during his career playing with renowned trumpet player Miles Davis, amongst other jazz greats. His legacy continues at the **St John Coltrane African Orthodox Church** in San Francisco.

Galvanized by the words on the liner notes of Coltrane's seminal *A Love Supreme,* in which he acknowledged his gratitude for emerging from the shadows of addiction, praised God, and asked to be 'given the means and privilege to make others happy through music,' this welcoming church anointed Coltrane as its patron saint. It is through Coltrane's words and music that the church finds its union with God.

Mass at St John's is celebrated every Sunday from noon to 3pm, and consists of confession, the Coltrane liturgy, scripture readings, hymns, spirituals, and preaching. All who attend are encouraged to participate and 'get your praise on' by singing, clapping, and dancing along, and by bringing instruments to play. Soulful, uninhibited jazz jams erupt in the intimate storefront space, and whatever your

> **GOSPEL BRUNCH**
> If you are seeking some soul food with your salvation, **1300 Fillmore** (tel: 415-771-7100; 11am and 2pm seatings; map D6), on the next block, serves a Gospel brunch where you can feast on scrambled eggs and grits or eggs Benedict and biscuits with gravy while listening to gospel songs and inspirational contemporary music – think John Lennon's *Imagine* and Bill Withers's *Lean on Me*.

religious proclivities might be, you are sure to be stirred by the infectious spirit of this church.

St John Coltrane African Orthodox Church; 1286 Fillmore Street; tel: 415-673-7144; www.coltranechurch.org; Sun noon–3pm; map D6

Chat up locals at **Nopa**, then hit up **cool bars** in the 'hood

In recent years, some popular San Francisco restaurants have steered a trend toward counter/bar service and communal tables – a boon to singles, travelers, and anyone who does not have a reservation.

The community table at **Nopa** (560 Divisidero Street; tel: 415-864-8643; map C8) serves a full dinner menu and is available on a first-come, first-served basis. It's a great place to meet people while indulging in organic 'urban rustic' cuisine. Nopa specializes in simple food sourced locally, cooked in their wood-burning oven and on the rotisserie.

Once you've chatted up the locals, it's time to move on to the bar scene in the burgeoning **NoPa** (North of the Panhandle) neighborhood. You'll find a treasure trove of groovy new bars, as well as stalwarts that have been around for decades.

For après-dinner sweets there is **Candybar** (1335 Fulton Street; tel: 415-673-7078; map C7), the city's seductively lit 'dessert lounge' and wine bar. Around the corner, cozy **Bar 821** (821 Divisidero Street; tel: 415-596-3986; map C7) serves beer, wine, and champagne cocktails (no full bar), but has plenty of local street cred and hosts art exhibitions.

Across the street, **Fly Bar** (762 Divisidero Street; tel: 415-931-4359; map C7) could use a facelift, but retains a core of diehard regulars thanks to its Happy Hour and savories like chicken and goat cheese quesadillas. Another establishment without a full liquor license, they make specialty drinks with sake and Korean *soju*.

Minibar (837 Divisadero Street; tel: 415-525-3565; map C7) boasts cheap drinks, cool art on the walls, a full bar, and an easygoing neighborhood vibe.

Immerse yourself in **Victorian architecture** on a tour starting at the **'Painted Ladies'**

Despite earthquakes, fire, and changing tastes, Victorian architecture still abounds in San Francisco. The highest concentration of these ornate, wood-framed 19th-century houses exists in the central neighborhoods west of Van Ness Avenue.

This tour begins on Alamo Square, bounded by Steiner, Fulton, Scott, and Hayes streets. Two different Victorian styles are most prevalent here. Queen Anne features multiple balconies, porches, turrets, curved windows, and spindlework; stick Victorians are identified by vertical lines, square bay windows, and adjoining front doors.

Most renowned are the **Painted Ladies of Alamo Square** (710–720 Steiner Street; map D7; *pictured*).

Also known as the 'Seven Sisters', these oft-photographed houses overlook the square on the eastern slope. With the backdrop of City Hall, the Transamerica Pyramid, and the downtown skyline, it is easy to see why this strip of Queen Anne Victorians is held in such fond regard.

Walking north past the Painted Ladies, you can see some good examples at nos. 818, 850, and 1043 Steiner. Stop at 1057 Steiner at Golden Gate Avenue and marvel at the lavishly ornate **Chateau Tivoli** (map D7), a Victorian townhouse that is now a bed-and-breakfast.

Double back and return to the corner of Steiner and Fulton streets. While not Victorian, the **French Second Empire** building (1000 Fulton Street; map D7),

GUIDED TOURS

If guided tours are more your thing, the **Victorian Home Walk** (tel: 415-252-9485; www.victorianwalk.com; charge) is a good option. Starting every day at Union Square at 11am, this 2½ hour tour travels Pacific Heights and other grandiose neighborhoods, and includes an inside tour of a Victorian house in the Queen Anne style. Alternatively, try a free City Guides tour (www.sfcityguides.org).

built in 1904 for San Francisco's second Archbishop, is worth seeing for its stately elegance.

Turn and walk West on Fulton to the remarkable and sinister **Westerfield House**, at 1198 Fulton at the corner of Scott (map C7). It was referred to by Tom Wolfe in *The Electric Kool-Aid Acid Test* as a 'shambling old Gothic house, a decayed giant, known as The Russian Embassy.' Not anymore. The house has been meticulously restored since Wolfe encountered it, sparing no detail.

Over in Pacific Heights are two more examples of Victorian architecure that you can actually enter. The **Haas-Lilienthal House** (2007 Franklin Street; tel: 415-441-3004; Sun 11am–4pm, Wed and Sat noon–3pm; charge; map E4) is an intact example of an upper-middle-class home of the period. A few blocks away, the **Octagon House** (2645 Gough Street; tel: 415-441-75120; map D3) was built in 1861 and named for its eight-sided cupola. It houses a museum open a few days a month to view the collection of historical documents from the Colonial and Federal periods.

Your tour concludes by viewing one of the city's most curious architectural mishmashes at nearby 2963 Webster Street (map D3). This hodgepodge of divergent decorative styles has a castle-like tower, Moorish arches, medieval parapets, Queen Anne Victorian elements, and is crowned with an onion-shaped dome like those on Russian Orthodox church

Satisfy your **shoe fetish** and swing by a designer's atelier in **hip Hayes Valley**

Two decades ago, **Hayes Valley** was a dodgy, crime-ridden area in the shadow of a grimy elevated freeway. The demolition of that freeway after the 1989 earthquake ushered in radical changes, and Hayes Valley has been reborn as a cute, artsy shopping district. Liquor stores and dive bars gave way to funky-chic boutiques; art galleries and eateries line leafy streets and alleys; and a green space displaying public art makes a refreshing gathering place.

For footwear fanatics, **Bulo** is best. From sandals and loafers to pumps and boots, Bulo's eclectic collection is a blend of handmade products, eco-friendly footwear, Italian boutique labels, and American- and Brazilian-made shoes.

Next door, **Gimme Shoes** (*pictured*) sells Italian-made designer styles for men and women in the latest foot fashions as dictated by Milan and New York, as well as leather bags, belts, and jewelry by local artists.

For an uber-creative shopping experience, swing by **Lemon Twist**, owned by a husband-and-wife team. She's a designer, he's an artist. Step into the quirky, inviting shop, painted bright turquoise with stenciled walls, which also serves as a workshop piled with bolts of fabric. The 1960s- and 1970s-inspired designs include mod dresses with round pockets, trenches with outstitching, and cool graphic tees. All are fresh, clever, and expertly tailored. Any design you see in the shop can be made into a garment in your choice of fabric.

Bulo; 418 Hayes Street; map E7
Gimme Shoes; 416 Hayes Street; map E7
Lemon Twist; 537 Octavia Boulevard; map E7

Sip wine in a **secluded back garden** or coffee on a sunny **sidewalk table**

The transformation of **Hayes Valley** from seedy, marginal neighborhood to bastion of hipness would not be complete without some great places to have coffee, tea, or a glass of wine. And after all that shopping, you might be inclined to stop for a beverage.

If you're all about the coffee, head to **Blue Bottle** (315 Linden Street; tel: 415-252-7535; map E7). Tucked away in a humble kiosk in an alley, this place has taken the city by storm with its dedication and precision in producing its celebrated 'artisan microroasted' brew.

If you're looking for the perfect almond croissant to accompany your coffee or tea and a sunny outdoor table in the midst of the action, **La Boulangerie** (500 Hayes Street; tel: 415-863-3376; map E7) delivers the goods. There are several locations sprinkled around the city, with bright-blue facades and tasty pastries and savories.

On the fence between coffee and tea or beer and wine? Stroll to **Momi Toby's Revolution Café and Art Bar** (528 Laguna Street; tel: 415-626-1508; map E7). They offer all of the above, as well as art on the walls and a laidback bohemian vibe.

If wine is the elixir of choice and people-watching the mission, an outdoor table at **Absinthe** (398 Hayes Street; tel: 415-551-1590; map E7) is sheer perfection on a sunny afternoon. Conversely, those looking to sip champagne in a secluded place away from the bustle should duck into the romantic back garden of **Arlequin** (384 Hayes Street; tel: 415-626-1211; map E7), with its flagstone terrace, wrought-iron cafe tables and arching vines of wisteria.

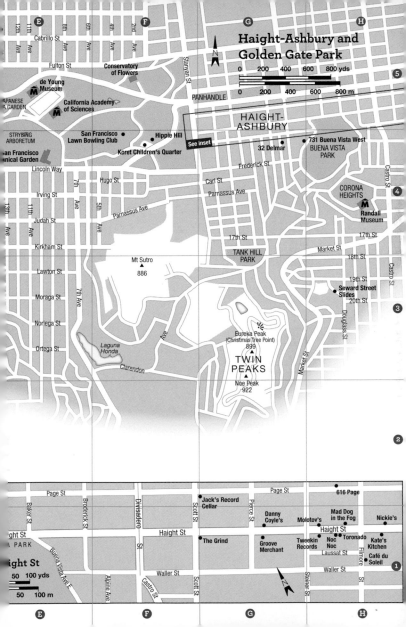

Haight-Ashbury and Golden Gate Park

N

| 0 | 200 | 400 | 600 | 800 yds |
| 0 | 200 | 400 | 600 | 800 m |

Cabrillo St

Fulton St

Conservatory of Flowers

de Young Museum

California Academy of Sciences

JAPANESE TEA GARDEN

STRYBING ARBORETUM

San Francisco Botanical Garden

San Francisco Lawn Bowling Club

Koret Children's Quarter

Hippie Hill

PANHANDLE

HAIGHT-ASHBURY

See inset

32 Delmar

731 Buena Vista West

BUENA VISTA PARK

Frederick St

Lincoln Way

Hugo St

Carl St

Parnassus Ave

CORONA HEIGHTS

Randall Museum

Irving St

Judah St

Kirkham St

Parnassus Ave

17th St

17th St

Lawton St

Mt Sutro
886

TANK HILL PARK

Market St

18th St

19th St

Seward Street Slides

20th St

Moraga St

Noriega St

Ortega St

Laguna Honda

Clarendon

Eureka Peak
(Christmas Tree Point)
899

TWIN PEAKS

Noe Peak
922

Douglass St

Market St

Castro St

Page St

Page St

616 Page

Jack's Record Cellar

Danny Coyle's

Molotov's

Mad Dog in the Fog

Nickie's

Baker St

Broderick St

Divisadero St

Haight St

Haight St

Haight St

The Grind

Groove Merchant

Tweekin Records

Noc Noc

Toronado

Laussat St

Kate's Kitchen

Café du Soleil

Waller St

Waller St

ight St

BUENA VISTA PARK

Buena Vista Ave E

Alpine Ave

Castro St

Scott St

Pierce St

Steiner St

Fillmore St

| 50 | 100 yds |
| 50 | 100 m |

N

E   F   G   H

Expand your horizons at **Amoeba Music**, the world's largest **independent music store**

The Haight-Ashbury was ground zero for the Summer of Love in 1967 and the psychedelic San Francisco sound, and the area's history has been intertwined with music ever since.

With online music driving a stake into the heart of corporate chain stores worldwide, innovative and independent retailers have thrived, and none more than the Taj Mahal of music stores, **Amoeba Music**. Anchoring the western terminus of Haight Street, in a cavernous former bowling alley, Amoeba offers seemingly endless new and used CDs, vinyl, and DVDs, intelligently categorized by genre, with extensive selections of hip-hop, electronica, jazz, rock, folk, and experimental music.

But Amoeba is more than a record shop. They offer great deals on used discs, listening stations, incredibly knowledgeable staff, vintage posters, and frequent in-store performances and signings by well-known bands.

Up and down Haight Street you can see people carrying their telltale bright yellow bags, but Amoeba isn't the only game in town. Five blocks east on Haight are **Recycled Records** (1377 Haight Street; tel: 415-626-4075; map C1), with a fine selection of used and rare items, and **Ceiba Records** (1364 Haight Street; tel: 415-437-9598; map D1), specializing in electronica.

Lower Haight offers even more variety – **Tweekin Records** (593 Haight Street; tel: 415-626-6995; map H1) and **Groove Merchant** (687 Haight Street; tel: 415-252-5766; map G1) are DJ paradises, while **Jack's Record Cellar** (254 Scott Street; tel: 415-431-3047; map G2) has the greatest collection of vintage vinyl in the city.

Amoeba Music; 1855 Haight Street; tel: 415-831-1200; www.amoeba.com; map A1

Hike to the top of **Buena Vista Park** on a fog-shrouded morning

One of the underappreciated treasures of Haight Street is gorgeous **Buena Vista Park**, a peaceful retreat in the center of the city.

The oldest park in San Francisco (dating from 1867) is on a steep hill that peaks at 575ft, and covers 37 acres. The summit, with its outstanding views, became popular with both visitors and residents, and during the 1906 earthquake people gathered here for five days to watch the city burn.

Thanks to the forestation efforts of John McLaren, the Scottish horticulturist who also supervised the planning and development of Golden Gate Park, secluded passageways wend through thick foliage and trees to the top.

The park has weathered some turbulent times over the years. During the Summer of Love, it became a haven for drug-dealing; in later years it was known as a gay cruising area. But since the late 1980s, the park has been cleaned up, a playground was built, and the tennis courts revamped.

Today, Buena Vista is populated with dogs and their owners, urban hikers and canoodling couples. On a foggy morning, the park takes on a mysterious beauty, like a landscape in a Tolkien story. You are rewarded for climbing to the park's summit by views that live up to its name, particularly its northern prospects of the Golden Gate Bridge and Marin Headlands.

Buena Vista Park; map H4, E1

117

Drink in the **nightlife** at the bars and clubs lining **Haight Street**

Haight Street is legendary for its rollicking nightlife, with bars for every taste – from the highfalutin Alembic to the lowbrow Toronado, and plenty more in between.

The **Alembic** (no. 1725; tel: 415-666-0822) suffers from an identity crisis: it likes to think it's a velvet-rope nightclub in Manhattan's Meatpacking District, but if you do get past the hostess, they have impressive cocktails and a creative food menu, while **Toronado** (no. 547; tel: 415-863-2276) on the other end of the street is known for its vast beer selection and a decidedly more laidback vibe.

Holding up the middle on Haight Street are two solid Irish bars, **Martin Macks** (no. 1568; tel: 415-861-2236) and **Danny Coyle's** (no. 668; tel: 415-558-8375). Classy **Bia** (no. 1640; tel: 415-861-8868)

is a wine bar/restaurant with an outdoor patio in back. The **Aub Zam Zam Room** (no. 1633; tel: 415-861-2545), formerly known for its Martini-only policy and persnickety owner, is now a groovy low-lit bar with top-drawer cocktails and Persian-accented decor. **Hobson's Choice** (no. 1601; tel: 415-621-5859) has a Victorian parlor feel, potent punch and a cozy upstairs nook. **Magnolia** (no. 1398; tel: 415-864-7468) is a gastropub and brewery with good beer specials like $3 Tuesdays. Locals' favorite dive the **Gold Cane** (no. 1569; tel: 415-626-1112) has a patio for smokers. There is a great jukebox and a pool table at grungy **Murio's Trophy Room** (no. 1811; tel: 415-752-2971). Gay bar **Trax** (no. 1437; tel: 415-864-4213) is friendly, dark, and offers cheap

drink specials. Funky **Noc Noc** (no. 557; tel: 415-861-5811) is known for nightly DJs and surrealist decor but doesn't have a license to serve hard liquor – beer, wine, and sake cocktails only. Sporty **Mad Dog in the Fog** (no. 530; tel: 415-550-7510), with an overabundance of blaring televisions, teems with an international crowd of soccer supporters, and **Molotov's** (no. 582; tel: 415-558-8019) is the place to go for tattooed hipsters, a pool table, and pinball. And this is just the bar scene.

For something extra with your cocktail, there are a few eclectic options on the Haight. Shabby-chic **Club Deluxe** (no. 1509; tel: 415-552-6949) has a retro Rat Pack vibe and draws a hip, stylish crowd. Deluxe hosts a weekly comedy night on Monday that has attracted some big names in alternative comedy. They also offer live music in the small lounge area, typically jazz, swing, and bossa nova. And for a taste of vaudeville, check out Little Minsky's monthly burlesque variety show.

One of the best north of Market Street dance clubs is **Milk Bar** (no. 1840; tel: 415-387-6455), with a different scene every night of the week, from a trippy Grateful Dead party to the 1980s-themed Culture Clash night to a long-running reggae/dance party with plenty of hip-hop in between.

Lastly, **Nickie's** (no. 466; tel: 415-235-0300) mixes it up with DJ nights, live traditional Irish music during brunch, karaoke Tuesdays, and a weekly pub quiz.

Haight Street; map A1-H1

Breakfast with hungover hipsters on **the Haight**

Haight Street is a late night kind of place, so it is not surprising that early mornings are generally mellow. But by about 10 or 11am, last night's partiers begin to rouse, hungover and hungry. Fortunately there are plenty of options for strong coffee and greasy fare. Some places even serve breakfast all day. Weekends can be crowded at brunch, but you could always get up early to beat the crowd. Or not.

Portions at **All You Knead** (no. 1466; tel: 415-552-4550) are huge, the menu is extensive, and prices are reasonable. Closet-sized **Pork Store Café** (no. 1451; tel: 415-864-6981; *pictured*) has lots of creative egg specialties and some healthy options. It gets packed, though – there are often lines out the door. **Squat and Gobble** (no. 1428; tel:

415-864-8484) does all the standard breakfast faves as well as delicious crepes, and they have a small back patio. **The Grind** (no. 783; tel: 415-864-0955) on mid-Haight has decadent breakfast choices like buttermilk pancakes with Nutella, and both indoor and outdoor seating. **Kate's Kitchen** (no. 471; tel: 415-626-3984) offers breakfast with a southern twist in a funky ambience. Try the French toast orgy, heaped with fruit and yogurt.

Slightly off Haight, **Café du Soleil** (200 Fillmore Street; tel: 415-934-8637) is a sunny, family-owned French cafe offering fresh-baked pastries, homemade granola, Sunday brunch specials, outdoor tables, and a congenial atmosphere.

Haight Street; map C1–H1

Locate the **Grateful Dead house** and **Janis Joplin's apartment** in Haight-Ashbury

Lots of people passed through the upper Haight during the wild days and nights of the late 1960s, and some made lasting impressions. Don some fringe and sandals, put a flower in your hair, and follow the footsteps of the musicians and other notables associated with this area.

Start at the cradle of the counterculture, the famous corner of Haight and Ashbury, and head west to 1524 Haight Street (map C1) to see guitar virtuoso Jimi Hendrix's crash pad. Reverse direction, walk back to Ashbury Street, and turn right to no. 635 (*pictured;* map C1), Janis Joplin's best-known residence (another of Joplin's homes is nearby on 122 Lyon Street). On the next block, the big Victorian at no. 710 (map C1), just south of Waller Street, was occupied by members of the Grateful Dead early in their careers. Across the street at no. 719 is the former headquarters of the notorious Hells Angels motorcycle club.

Walk up the block to Frederick Street, turn left, then proceed one half-block to Delmar Street and take a left. No. 32 (map G4) is where Sid Vicious non-fatally overdosed after the last Sex Pistols show. Return south up the hill to Frederick,

proceed east to Masonic Avenue (one block past Ashbury) and turn left. At no. 1235 (map C1) is the Symbionese Liberation Army safe-house, where heiress, actress, and abductee Patty Hearst was hidden. Turn and head up Masonic, back to Frederick, and turn left, go one block, and then turn left again onto Buena Vista West. At no. 731 (map G4) Graham Nash of Crosby, Stills, Nash & Young lived, and several owners later, Bobby McFerrin.

Not in the immediate vicinity but northeast of Haight Street, at 616 Page Street (map H2) between Fillmore and Steiner, was the headquarters of Charles Manson and the Manson Family.

Delve into the racks of **vintage shops** and thrift stores for a **retro look**

There is definitely a San Francisco style. The weather – cool mornings, warm afternoons, and chilly nights – dictates that dressing in layers and accessorizing with scarves and hats is often the way to stay comfortable while looking good. As San Franciscans are expert recyclers (it is the law here), there is a tendency to mix new pieces with vintage or thrift-store finds, creating signature styles.

If you are looking to add something new to your wardrobe, why not look for something old? Haight Street has a trove of vintage and thrift stores. Here are a few places to jumpstart a thrift-shopping spree.

Crossroads Trading Co. (no. 1519) sells on-trend clothing in excellent condition. Think dark-colored skinny jeans, men's graphic tees and romantic floral dresses. Organized by era, color, and theme, **Held Over** (no. 1543) makes it easier to find 1970s hip huggers or cocktail dresses from the 1950s. The constantly rotating inventory at **Buffalo Exchange** (no. 1555) includes designer labels, vintage items, jeans, leather, current basics, brand-new merchandise, and accessories. Follow the pulsing tunes into uber-hip **Wasteland** (no. 1660) for motorcycle jackets, cashmere, preppy classics, faux, and fur. Elegant **La Rosa Vintage Boutique** (no. 1711) is an upscale vintage shop specializing in dresses and formal wear.

Haight Street; map B1–C1

Revel in expansive views of the city, the bay, and beyond on **Twin Peaks**

In a city of awe-inspiring vistas, the ultimate money shot goes to the mind-blowing view from Twin Peaks.

Close to the geographical center of San Francisco, **Twin Peaks** is named for the two summits that at 922ft are the second-highest peaks after Mount Davidson to the south. There is no public transportation to the top, and the signage to get there is spotty, but the view at the end (*pictured*) is worth persevering for – encompassing Mount Diablo to the east, the bay and entire downtown skyline, and a sliver of the Pacific to the northwest.

Nearby you'll find some other worthy treks with stunning views. **Tank Hill**, accessed from a small staircase off Twin Peaks Boulevard near Crown Terrace to the south, or at the top of Stanyan Street just beyond Belgrave Avenue to the north, is a rocky outcrop of undeveloped land that once contained a drinking-water storage tank. Small paths among fields of wildflowers lead to the circular imprint of the former tank. This is a fun hike from upper Haight or Cole Valley.

East of Tank Hill on **Corona Heights**, another magnificent view awaits. Here you will discover a community garden, a children's playground, and a 60-foot sheer rock wall. Uphill toward the peak, corkscrew around hills that open up to barbecue pits, tennis courts, and breathtaking vistas.

The **Randall Museum** sits atop this lofty crest and focuses on arts, crafts, sciences, and natural history for children. Exhibits include live animals, an interactive discovery zone, and a fascinating transparent Plexiglas beehive.

Twin Peaks; map G3
Tank Hill; map G4
Corona Heights; map H4
Randall Museum; 199 Museum Way; tel: 415-554-9600; www.randallmuseum.org; Tue–Sat 10am–5pm; free; map H4

Experience a **rainforest**, an aquarium, or a planetarium at the **California Academy of Sciences**

The newest museum on the block, the **California Academy of Sciences** opened in 2008 in a masterpiece of sustainable architecture that was 10 years in the making. The wait was worth it. With an aquarium, planetarium, natural history museum, and even a rainforest, the cutting-edge project is topped by an extraordinary 'living roof' seeded with a canopy of native plants that provide a habitat for wildlife.

Venture inside and be wowed by the natural world that unfolds around you. The aquarium itself is home to 38,000 live animals from around the globe. Come nose-to-jaw with a phenomenal albino alligator as it slithers around in an underwater swamp exhibit.

On the first floor, head upward through the rainforest exhibit that ascends four stories on a spiraling ramp, allowing you to get up close to bats from Borneo, chameleons from Madagascar, and free-flying Costa Rican birds and butterflies all housed beneath a glass dome.

Once you emerge from the humid rainforest, head to the planetarium and space out in the most accurate and interactive digital universe ever created. Shows have included tours of the universe, supernova explosions, and NASA feeds.

If all this science gets you hungry, the **Academy Café** offers a multicultural menu of paninis, spring rolls, and tacos, and the **Moss Room** is a fine-dining restaurant featuring California and Mediterranean cuisine.

California Academy of Sciences; 55 Music Concourse Drive in Golden Gate Park; tel: 415-379-8000; www.cal academy.org; Mon–Sat 9.30am–5pm, Sun 11am–5pm; charge; map E5

Jam to the beats on **Hippie Hill** or mount a horse on a **vintage carrousel**

The southeast corner of Golden Gate Park is devoted to play – and kids and adults alike can get their groove on here.

Near the park entrance at Haight and Stanyan streets is a sunny, southern-facing slope known as **Hippie Hill**, actually part of **Sharon Meadow**. This has been a gathering spot for a freeform improvisational drum circle for decades. People of all ages, races, and backgrounds drop in with percussion instruments for an unstructured jam. You are likely to see hippie girls dancing, homeless people joining the fun, folks playing Frisbee, and sunbathers soaking up rays to the backdrop of beats as the smell of marijuana permeates the air. Sharon Meadow has been an important gathering space for musicians since the Summer of Love in 1967, and remains part of the hippie scene.

Nearby, a delightful 1912 carrousel, carved with a colorful menagerie of animals, is part of the **Koret Children's Quarter** that was completely overhauled in 2007. The new playground has two sets of play structures for children of different ages, a sand area, and a water feature. Slippery concrete slides built into the hillside are a remnant from the original playground – for maximum thrill they are best used with cardboard.

Locals' tip: fans of concrete slides will have a blast hurtling down the **Seward Street slides**, a little-known and difficult-to-find spot at Douglass and Seward streets in the Castro (Seward is between 19th and 20th streets, map H3).

Hippie Hill and Koret Children's Corner; Golden Gate Park; map F4

Paddle around **Stow Lake**, then **visit the bison** that live in Golden Gate Park

For a lovely way to spend a few hours, make your way to the **Boathouse at Stow Lake** and relax on a tranquil lake in the pristine surrounds of Golden Gate Park.

Off John F. Kennedy Drive, west of the de Young Museum (*p.127*) and behind the Japanese Tea Garden (*p.128*), you will happen upon the Rustic Bridge that leads up to **Strawberry Hill**, an island in the middle of the lake. The short hike offers views of a waterfall,

the Chinese pavilion (a gift from Taipei that was shipped in several thousand pieces and assembled in 1981, *pictured*), and the city from the top.

The Boathouse is on the northwest corner of the lake. Here you can picnic, feed the ducks, or rent bicycles or boats for a leisurely cruise. The concession here is a bit antiquated, offering only pink popcorn, hot dogs, ice cream, and soda, but paddling around the lake beneath graceful arched stone bridges is a pleasant way to enjoy the park that could be either romantic or a treat for children, depending.

If you are up for more adventure, continue west in the park past **Lindley Meadow** to **Spreckels Lake**. Stop and watch hobbyists launch little model yachts in the placid water. Just beyond is the **Buffalo Paddock**, where a herd of American bison roam, a living memorial to the Wild West. Catching these magnificent beasts silhouetted by fog is an unforgettable image.

The Boathouse at Stow Lake; Stow Lake Drive in Golden Gate Park; tel: 415-752-0347; daily 10am–4pm; charge; map D5

Immerse yourself in an **art extravaganza** at Friday nights at the **de Young**

The ultramodern building with the copper facade in Golden Gate Park belongs to the **de Young**, one of the city's great fine-art museums, showcasing American art from the 17th–20th centuries and native works from the Americas, Africa, and the Pacific. The cutting-edge building opened in 2005, replacing the museum's former home that was damaged in the 1989 Loma Prieta earthquake. Copper was chosen for the building's 'skin' due to its changeable quality – as it oxidizes it will assume a rich patina that will blend gracefully into the leafy park setting.

Try to schedule your visit to the de Young on Friday evening, when the museum stays open late and offers a variety of interdisciplinary arts programs with changing themes. The festive atmosphere

includes live music, dance, poetry, films, tours, and lectures. Hands-on art-making activities are available for children and adults. The cafe and a cocktail bar are open for dinner and drinks, with a special Friday night menu. Regular admission prices apply if you want to visit the de Young's galleries, but the special events are free.

The permanent collection is worth a look, to see John Singer Sargent's paintings, priceless murals from Teotihuacan, a carved Eskimo mask, and a Makonde helmet mask from Mozambique.

De Young Museum; 50 Hagiwara Tea Garden Drive; tel: 415-750-3600; http:// deyoung.famsf.org; Tue-Sun 9.30am-5.15pm, mid-Jan-Nov Fri until 8.45pm; charge, Fri night programs free; map E5

TOWER AND CAFE
If you don't have time for a proper visit to the galleries at the de Young, stop by and take the elevator to the top of the observation tower. It is free, and the 360-degree view from this vantage point in the middle of the park is fantastic. Or lunch at the **de Young Café**, an acclaimed restaurant with a 'farm to fork' philosophy – all ingredients are sourced within 150 miles of the kitchen.

Release your inner botanist at three of Golden Gate Park's **gorgeous gardens**

Golden Gate Park is not only San Francisco's playground but also an urban oasis. At just over 1,000 acres, it is home to nine lakes, two waterfalls, 200 species of birds, and 10 gardens.

Cloistered behind high wooden walls and a Shinto gate is the most celebrated of these gardens, the lushly sculpted and meticulously designed **Japanese Tea Garden**. Within this Zen sanctuary are flowering cherry, maple, and bonsai trees, a round moon bridge arching over goldfish ponds, bronze Buddhas, elaborately carved pagodas, stone pathways, and sculptures hidden in little nooks.

Take a leisurely wander through the garden, stopping to rest on stone benches and admire the plants and flowers, many imported from Japan. Then head to the teahouse and choose from a variety of teas including green, oolong, and jasmine while nibbling Japanese cookies.

East of the Japanese Tea Garden, close to the park's Stanyan Street entrance, is the **Conservatory of Flowers**. The whitewashed wood and glass greenhouse is a Victorian confection filled with rare, exotic plants and tropical flowers. Rainbow-colored light dapples the interior through stained glass.

The Conservatory features four permanent galleries – aquatic plants, highland tropics, lowland tropics, and potted plants – each painstakingly cared for by nursery specialists. Plants are rotated into the galleries as they bloom, so visitors will always see the plants in the collection at their peak.

Past special exhibits include topics like butterflies and carnivorous plants. The adjacent dahlia garden is truly a wonder in late summer and fall.

Across the park to the south, the magnificent **San Francisco Botanical Garden** at **Strybing Arboretum** houses more than 8,000 species of plants, separated by climate and country of origin, from New Zealand to Chile, and connected by a looped boardwalk path. Stroll around the world through a redwood grove, a primitive plant collection, a Mesoamerican cloud garden, and among Cape Province aloes and Peruvian lilies. Make sure to breathe deeply in the garden of fragrance, designed for the visually impaired, and pay a visit to the celestial Japanese moon-viewing garden. There are also amazing succulents, a butterfly garden, and a California natives section.

Daily guided tours are free, and you can call ahead to reserve tours with a specific focus.

Japanese Tea Garden; 7 Hagiwara Tea Garden Drive; tel: 415-666-3232; daily Mar–Oct 9am–6pm, Nov–Feb 9am–4.45pm; charge, free before 10am; map E5
Conservatory of Flowers; 100 John F. Kennedy Drive; tel: 415-831-2090; Tue–Sun 9am–5pm; charge; map F5
San Francisco Botanical Garden; 1199 9th Avenue; tel: 415-661-1316; Mon–Fri 8am–4.30pm, Sat–Sun and holidays 10am–5pm; free; map E4

Brandish a **bow and arrow** for an afternoon of **sporting leisure**

Golden Gate Park offers lots of opportunities for recreation – tennis courts, a baseball field, jogging paths, and even a polo field. But why not try something a little more adventurous, yet not too strenuous?

Archery is the ultimate leisure sport. You don't work up a sweat, so you stay looking fresh, but it improves concentration, coordination, and form. It can be social or it can be solo. Best of all, you can enjoy a day outdoors in the park.

Tucked away in the northwest corner of Golden Gate Park behind the Dutch Windmill is the small **Golden Gate Archery Range**, with a line of hay bales. It is free to use, but you need to rent equipment. Fortunately, two nearby shops can provide you with everything you need. The **San Francisco Archery Pro Shop** will suit you up in the necessary gear – bow, arrows, and targets – and give lessons. They will even accompany you to the range. **Cupid's Gate Archery** rents super high-end gear and gives private lessons on safety and shooting instruction. They also host a Saturday archery clinic.

If even a spot of archery is too fast-paced for you, then a leisurely

game of lawn bowling might be more your speed. Take a lesson from a seasoned member of the **San Francisco Lawn Bowling Club** at noon on Wednesdays and Saturdays, and try your skills on the bowling green.

Golden Gate Archery Range; 47th Avenue near Fulton Street; tel: 415-751-2776; map A5
San Francisco Archery Pro Shop; 3795 Balboa Street; tel: 415-751-2776; www.bysel.com/sfarch; map B5
Cupid's Gate Archery; 944 47th Avenue; tel: 415-336-6512; www.cupidsgatearchery.com; map A5
San Francisco Lawn Bowling Club; near Sharon Meadow; tel: 415-487-8787; map F4

Enjoy a **meal and a brew** with a view at a landmark **Deco building**

On the edge of Golden Gate Park, near the shores of the Pacific, the Beach Chalet is one of a precious few places in the city where you can sit down for a meal, a drink, and a view of the ocean.

In a landmark building that blends the Art Deco and Arts and Crafts styles of the 1930s, the **Beach Chalet Brewery & Restaurant** sits above a visitor's center that showcases wood-carvings, mosaics, and historic murals that capture the flavor of San Francisco during that period.

Here you can gaze out over the crashing surf of **Ocean Beach** while sipping ale from the on-premises brewery. The menu is a mix of pub food and fine dining, with an emphasis on seafood. It's popular with the brunch crowd, who come for classic fare with a few twists, like crab Benedict and a Monte Cristo sandwich.

If you can't score a window seat, check out the **Park Chalet**, the

> **BAY TO BREAKERS**
> The zany Bay to Breakers footrace on the third Sunday of May begins at the Embarcadero and ends at the Great Highway near Ocean Beach. Costumes are encouraged, alcohol is tolerated (just don't flaunt it), and nudity is expected. Serious runners join gorilla suits, 10-people-long centipedes and themed floats for $7\frac{1}{2}$ miles across the city, creating a moving metaphor for San Francisco.

sister restaurant in back facing **Golden Gate Park**. Here you can feast on small plates, delicious salads, and pizzas. Eat and drink inside, on the patio or the lawn, while listening to free live surf music, family concerts or jam bands on weekend afternoons, and jazz and lounge on Tuesday and Friday evenings.

Beach Chalet Brewery & Restaurant and Park Chalet; 1000 Great Highway at Ocean Beach; tel: 415-386-8439; daily B, L, & D; map A5

Mission and Castro

Chow a **burrito** at a **Mission taqueria**

For a quick, cheap, and delicious meal that will keep you sated for hours, duck into one of the many taquerias in the Mission. Stand in line, cafeteria-style, and customize your own tortilla-wrapped meal.

Tortillas are warmed, then filled with your choice of *carnitas* (pork), *carne asada* (steak), *pollo* (chicken), or *camarones* (shrimp), plus cheese, Spanish rice, beans, and salsa. You might opt to upgrade to a 'super' with sour cream and guacamole. Meatless versions are also pretty satisfying. At most places, you get a handful of homemade tortilla chips on the side. Completing the experience is a cold glass of *horchata*, a sweet,

milky beverage made with rice and cinnamon, ladled from big jar behind the counter, or an *agua fresca*, a refreshing, fruity drink.

Ask any local and they will send you to their favorite joint, but some of the most popular are **La Taqueria** (2889 Mission Street; tel: 415-285-7117; map F1), **Le Cumbre** (515 Valencia; tel: 415-863-8205; map E4), **El Toro** (598 Valencia Street; tel: 415-431-3351; map E4), **Cancun** (2288 Mission Street; tel: 415-252-9560), **Pancho Villa** (3071 16th Street; tel: 415-864-8840), and **Papalote** (3409 24th Street; tel: 415-970-8815).

A tip: silverware is unnecessary. Keep your burrito wrapped in foil to hold it together and peel the foil back as you munch.

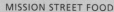

MISSION STREET FOOD

Locating the Mission's roving food carts is a fun culinary adventure. The **Magic Curry Kart**, serving red or green curry with chicken or tofu, is based near Linda and 19th streets. **Amuse Bouche**, manned by a Frenchman selling morning fare of chai, quiche, and muffins, can be found sporadically at Mission and 24th streets. The **Creme Brulee Guy** uses twitter.com (cremebruleecart) to inform of his whereabouts and daily flavors, like vanilla bean and lavender.

Shop for peg-legs and spy glasses at a **writing center** disguised as a **pirate shop**

The Mission has its share of unusual and compelling shops. For all of your sea-marauding needs, look no further than the **Pirate Store** at **826 Valencia**.

Here you will find eye patches, compasses, skull flags, and mermaid bait. The clever little shop has rotating art installations in its storefront window, and built-in cabinets and drawers to browse through for all things buccaneer-related.

The Pirate Store is more than just a safe haven for picaroons. It is the brainchild of San Francisco's literary darling Dave Eggers, author of *A Heartbreaking Work of Staggering Genius* and publisher of *McSweeney's*. 826 Valencia is a non-profit organization dedicated to supporting students aged 6–18 to develop their writing skills. Opening the kitschy pirate store was a necessity, since a city ordinance dictated that the space be used for retail.

The writing center offers free programs including tutoring, field trips, workshops, and student publishing. Eggers's literary journals and the students' work are on sale in the Pirate Store.

If the Pirate Store has got you primed for quirky retail, try the **Curiosity Shoppe** (855 Valencia Street; map E3), where you can pick up a mini Diana camera, a vintage telephone, or a ukulele; or hit **Paxton Gate** (824 Valencia Street; map E3) for the perfect fossil or butterfly engraving.

Pirate Store at 826 Valencia; tel: 415-642-5905; www.826valencia.org; daily noon–6pm; map E3

Find fresh **alternative theater** at **The Marsh**, a breeding ground for new performance

What Union Square is to mainstream theater, the Mission is to alternative. From one-woman shows to ensemble groups, a cluster of small, unique theaters are pushing the envelope, taking risks and reaping rewards.

One such risk-taker, **The Marsh** (1062 Valencia Street; tel: 826-5750; map E2), encourages dramatic entrepreneurship. Stand-up comic and media personality Brian Copeland workshopped *Not a Genuine Black Man* here before taking it to LA and off-Broadway.

The oldest alternative space in the city, **Intersection for**

the Arts (446 Valencia Street; tel: 415-626-2787; map E4) is home to resident theater group **Campo Santo**, which nurtures playwrights to create provocative new theatrical experiences.

Showcasing plays from the gay community, **Theatre Rhinoceros** (1360 Mission Street; tel: 552-4100; map E5) is the longest-running queer theater in the country. An innovator in San Francisco since 1977, the Rhino maintains its own production company.

Another niche theater, **Brava! for Women in the Arts** (2781 24th Street; tel: 415-641-7657; map G1) offers thought-provoking theater, music, and educational programs intended to celebrate feminism and multiculturalism – though not all of their productions ascribe to that agenda. Productions range from a one-man show probing questions of race, ethnicity, and homosexuality in hip-hop youth culture to a dark musical spoof on beauty, superficiality, and youth-obsessed culture.

The **Dark Room** (2263 Mission Street; tel: 415-401-7987) is a cozy, narrow theater whose repertoire leans heavily toward comedy. Look out for sketch comedy, improv, original works, and 'bad movie night' screenings.

Support a **grassroots culinary movement** while tasting good wine and cheese

In a small space on 18th and Guerrero, a community comes together through a common interest in food, wine, art, and sustainability. **18 Reasons** is the vision of a grocer who wanted more from his food. Sam Mogannam and his staff at **Bi-Rite Market** (p.146) founded the grass-roots organization in 2008 as an extension of the market's philosophy. The gist is to engage with the people who feed us – organic farmers, biodynamic vintners, chefs, bakers, cheesemakers, and fishermen.

On Thursday evenings at 7pm, 18 Reasons hosts **18th Hour**, an informal, moderately priced drop-in that usually involves a tasting. Events have focused on champagne, ice cream, a wine and goat cheese pairing with a Vermont cheesemaker, a mixologist demonstrating the latest trends in cocktails, and a tour of farm cheeses from the British Isles led by a representative from Neal's Yard Dairy. Come early, the space fills up.

The center also hosts community dinners and classes. They are also art aficionados and maintain a gallery that is open on Saturdays. Past exhibits have included an interactive installation on persimmons and Sita Bhaumik's examination of how spice evokes memory.

18 Reasons; 593 Guerrero Street; tel: 415-252-9816; www.18reasons.org; see website for calendar; charge; map E3

Go on a **bar crawl** in the **funky, diverse** Mission

After a busy day pounding the Mission streets, you'll be ready for a drink. Luckily there is no shortage of watering holes in this part of town.

Start at **Zeitgeist** (199 Valencia Street; tel: 255-7505; map E5), a rough-and-tumble biker hangout with an enormous outdoor patio filled with long picnic tables. Order a pitcher of beer, put some classic rock on the jukebox, and chill in the back.

Keeping with the outdoor theme, taxi over to **Medjool** (2522 Mission Street; tel: 415-550-9055; map E2) for a vastly different scene at one of San Francisco's few rooftop lounges. Sample Spanish wine and Mediterranean tapas while basking in the 360-degree panoramic view. Arrive early or be prepared to wait.

Next stop, **Beauty Bar** (2299 Mission Street; tel: 415-285-0323; map E3) for Martinis and manicures, kitschy fun, and a retro vibe in a retro-fitted beauty parlor that lures both Mission hipsters and Marina dwellers (two highly different breeds).

Next, head to the **Makeout Room** (3225 22nd Street; tel: 415-647-2888; map E2), a favorite spot with locals looking for a laidback venue with dark corners, a decent Happy Hour, live music, DJs, and moderate (if any) cover charges. Stop by to absorb authentic Mission-flavored nightlife.

Properly lubricated, wind down for the finale: a torchy sing-a-long at **Martuni's** (4 Valencia Street; tel: 415-241-0205; map E5). This velvet-draped piano bar attracts a mixed crowd of gay and straight crooners to belt out the words to show tunes and pop-music classics.

Experience **edgy artwork** at time-honored **Mission galleries**

The Mission is a hotbed of creativity, and a few galleries have been providing outlets for art – from political to experimental – for decades.

Since 1970, the tiny shopfront **Galería de la Raza** has fostered awareness and appreciation of Chicano and Latino art, mounting exhibitions and hosting poetry readings and workshops. The Digital Mural Project created by GDLR's Youth Media is a collage of images with references to the war in Iraq and local gang unrest.

Edgy Mission gallery and performance space **The Lab** has favored experimental boundary-crossing art by emerging artists since 1984. Events have included performances from sex educator and artist Annie Sprinkle and

Squart (Spontaneous Queer Art). Check to see if your visit coincides with their annual art auction for great prices on original works.

Nearby, in a cavernous space beneath a grungy freeway in SoMa, is **SoMarts**, born in 1979 and a supporter of art for and by the people, outside the circles of high culture. Today the Main Gallery exhibits the work of more than 1,000 Bay Area artists annually.

Galería de la Raza; 2857 24th Street; tel: 415-826-8009; Tue 1–7pm, Wed–Sat noon–6pm; free; map G1
The Lab; 2948 16th Street; tel: 415-864-8855; Wed–Sat 1–6pm during exhibitions; free; map F4
SoMarts Cultural Center; 934 Brannan Street; tel: 415-552-1770; Tue–Fri noon–7pm, Sat noon–5pm; free; map H5

OPEN STUDIOS
A unique way to experience San Francisco's art scene is by participating in **Open Studios**, which takes place every October. Doors all over the city are flung open and the public is invited inside to view work, sip wine, interact with artists, and buy art straight from the source. The heaviest concentration of studios is in the **Hunter's Point Shipyard**. Pick up the free guide and make a day of it – bopping around the shipyard and tapping into the creative pulse (www.artspan.org).

Tuck into a **California-style brunch** with a movie at **Foreign Cinema**

A meal at **Foreign Cinema** is a quintessential San Francisco experience. It combines culinary excellence, a cool industrial-chic space, an eclectic clientele, and an art-house cinema, all tucked away down a candlelit corridor in the middle of the grungy-hip Mission.

The ambience is unforgettable. The narrow corridor opens to a spacious covered outdoor courtyard, where at dusk films are projected onto the far wall. Concrete and exposed brick create a distinctly urban vibe outside, while indoors, the spare dining room is hung with clusters of bare bulbs suspended chandelier-like from 20ft ceilings.

A daily changing California/Mediterranean-inspired menu is offered seven nights a week, as well as a Saturday and Sunday brunch. While dinner is romantic, and you can enjoy Fellini or Antonioni with your curry-roast chicken and kale, brunch is legendary. Omelets are made with seasonal ingredients like sweet white corn and heirloom tomatoes, and the house-made 'pop tarts' are filled with that morning's fresh fruit. The raw bar has a selection of oysters, as well as clams, cooked shrimp, and Dungeness crab. A three-course children's tasting menu courts the wee ones.

Husband and wife chefs and owners Gayle Pirie and John Clark honed their culinary chops with longstanding tenures at **Zuni Café**, one of the city's groundbreaking restaurants embracing market-fresh California cuisine.

Foreign Cinema; 2534 Mission Street; tel: 415-648-7600; www.foreigncinema. com; Mon–Fri D, Sat–Sun Br & D; brunch around $35 per person, three courses, no alcohol; map E2

Roam around **24th Street** to take in the Mission's **magnificent murals**

Head to 24th Street to immerse yourself in the Latino-dominated heart of the Mission, where eye-catching murals cover buildings as far as the eye can see.

Stop first at the **Precita Eyes Mural Arts and Visitors Center**. Here you can pick up a pamphlet on the guided mural walks they offer, or purchase a $5 map showing 92 murals in the vicinity, with artists and titles on the back, and venture out on your own.

Weave in and out of side streets as you traverse 24th from Mission Street to York Street to be treated to vivid eye candy like *Sí Se Puede*, part of a stunning mural environment that covers César Chávez Elementary School on Shotwell Street.

Two blocks west from Precita Eyes, between Harrison and Folsom streets, is **Balmy Alley** (map G1), the mother lode of Mission mural art. Nearly every surface is painted with images, from the Virgin of Guadalupe to Social Realist depictions of immigration to an AIDS memorial.

Precita Eyes Mural Arts and Visitors Center; 2981 24th Street; tel: 415-285-2287; www.precitaeyes.org; Mon–Fri 10am–5pm Sat 10am–4pm, Sun noon–4pm; charge; map G1

Travel back in time at the **Mission Dolores**, the **oldest building** in the city

Built in 1791, the **Mission San Francisco de Asís** is the oldest standing structure in the city. It still remains intact after withstanding the test of time and two major earthquakes. A visit to the birthplace of the city is a fascinating journey through time.

The mission was founded by Father Juniperro Serra, a Franciscan monk, and later became known as **Mission Dolores** due to the proximity of a nearby lake, Arroyo de Nuestra Señora de los Dolores (Lake of our Lady of Sorrows). It is the sixth in a chain of missions that dot the California coastline.

Friar Font, a member of the original missionary expedition, wrote descriptively about the chosen spot:

We rode about one league to the east [from the Presidio], one to the east-southeast, and one to the southeast, going over hills covered with bushes, and over valleys of good land. We thus came upon two lagoons and several springs of good water, meanwhile encountering much grass, fennel, and other good herbs. When we arrived at a lovely creek, which because it was the Friday of Sorrows [the Friday before Palm Sunday], we called the Arroyo de los Dolores... On the banks of the Arroyo... we discovered many fragrant chamomiles and other herbs, and many wild violets. Near the streamlet the lieutenant planted a little corn and some garbanzos in order to try out the soil, which to us appeared good.

The humble mission included a simple chapel with solid 4ft thick walls built by Native Americans in a mixture of Spanish-colonial style and native construction methods. A gilded Baroque altarpiece was imported from Mexico.

Adorning the ceiling are paintings created by the natives based on Ohlone tribal designs using vegetable dye. The Ohlone were among the Costanoan tribes recruited by the missionaries in their quest to convert them to Catholicism. They were offered food and protection, and they entertained the *padres* by dancing cloaked in traditional garb, with shells, feathers, and body paint. Sadly, some historical reports indicate that the natives were mistreated by the *padres*, and many ran away.

Further tragedy ensued for the natives. Two measles epidemics in the early 19th century took the lives of thousands.

Masses are still held here, and a small museum displays historical photos and documents. Outside in the grounds, a pensive statue of Father Serra stands in the mission garden, and a ceramic mural graces an interior wall.

But most fascinating is the white-walled mission cemetery where the remains of the city's earliest *padres* are buried. Small and serene, with light slanting over the mission walls illuminating the headstones, the cemetery is hauntingly beautiful. It is no wonder that it was chosen as a film location by Alfred Hitchcock for the movie *Vertigo*. Look for a pedestal that reads 'In Prayerful Memory of our Faithful Indians,' acknowledging the Native Americans who died here.

Mission Dolores; 3321 16th Street; tel: 415-621-8203; www.missiondolores.org; daily 9am–4pm; donation suggested; map D4

145

Hit **Tartine Bakery** for goodies and catch some rays at **Dolores 'Beach'**

When the rest of the city is blanketed with fog, locals head to **Dolores Park** in the sun-drenched Mission. Affectionately referred to as Dolores 'Beach,' the park comprises 13 sloping acres of (mostly) green space with six tennis courts, a basketball court, soccer fields, and a playground, all bounded by Dolores, 20th, Church, and 18th streets.

Gorgeous views of downtown notwithstanding, Dolores is far from the city's prettiest park. But it has an allure that goes beyond physical beauty. Here, the city's communities gather in a feat of effortless self-segregation.

Dog-walkers claim space among Latino family revelers; gay men in Speedos sun themselves in one area, lesbians in another; Mission hipsters tend to collect in pockets near Dolores Park Café. There is a homeless area, a place for children, and a section where pot-smokers are virtually undisturbed.

Chilling at Dolores Beach is best with proper provisions. For mouthwatering treats both sweet and savory, stop first at the esteemed **Tartine Bakery**. **Bi-Rite Market** has everything else you need for a picnic, including organic fruits, cheeses, and alcohol. They also have a creamery across the street (3692 18th Street), selling ice cream, sorbet, and confections.

Dolores Park; map D3
Tartine Bakery; 600 Guerrero Street;
tel: 415-487-2600; map E3
Bi-Rite Market; 3639 18th Street; tel: 415-
241-9760; map D3

> **MOVIES IN THE PARK**
> From April through October, free movies are screened in Dolores Park on the second Thursday of each month. Bring a blanket, buy some popcorn, and scope out Virginia the Tamale Lady, selling her homemade husk-wrapped delectables.

Kick up your heels on the **dance floor** in the **Mission and Castro**

There are lots of opportunities to get your groove on in San Francisco. In the Mission and Castro neighborhoods, the lines between club, bar, restaurant, and lounge tend to blur. Boogie down on intimate dance floors, each with its own flavor.

El Rio (3158 Mission; tel: 415-282-3325; map F1; *pictured*) is a culturally, racially, and sexually mixed bar, with Salsa Sundays and global, rock, punk, and hip-hop dance parties other nights. Stop in for the BBQ on the back deck, then dance to the rhythm of diversity.

Castro hotspot **Q Bar** (456 Castro Street; tel: 415-864-2877; map B3) features high-energy DJ dance music every night, including Throwback Thursdays ('80s and '90s pop) and Tuesday Grrlz Nite. They also offer generous drink specials.

Elbo Room (647 Valencia Street; tel: 415-552-7788; map E3) has two levels – a relaxed downstairs bar scene with pool tables and an instant-photo booth, and a rocking upstairs lounge with live music and dancing, from punk and funk to rockabilly and salsa.

One of the grooviest dance parties in town is at **Little Baobab** (3388 19th Street; tel: 415-643-3558; map E3), a tiny Senegalese shoebox restaurant where DJs spin dancehall, Brazilian, Afrobeats, and reggaeton, and ginger-infused cocktails are strong and tasty.

Further afield, many of the big dance clubs – **1015 Folsom** (1015 Folsom Street; tel: 415-431-7444), **111 Minna** (111 Minna Street; tel: 415-974-1719), **Mezzanine** (444 Jessie Street; tel: 415-625-8880), and **Cat Club** (1190 Folsom Street; tel: 415-703-8965) are in SoMa. **Ruby Skye** (420 Mason Street; tel: 415-693-0777) and **Slide** (430 Mason Street; tel: 415-421-1916) are in the Tenderloin.

Catch a film or a Mary Poppins sing-a-long at a single-screen movie palace

As flamboyant and festive as the neighborhood it embodies, the single-screen **Castro Theatre** is a true old-time movie palace. Built in 1922, the lavish Spanish Baroque building has two dramatic staircases, Art Deco flourishes and a Wurlitzer pipe organ on an ascending platform. For a quintessential Castro experience, enjoy the frivolity of a camp sing-a-long to *The Sound of Music*, *Mary Poppins*, or *Grease*.

In the Mission, intellectuals can get their fill of political documentaries, film noir, and flicks about artists and musicians at **The Roxie Film Center**, the oldest continually running theater in San Francisco.

You'll find characterful cinemas all over San Francisco. Over in the Haight, sink into a comfy couch at the funky, worker-owned **Red Vic** for classics, cult films, and foreign and art-house titles. Or kick back with cocktails and appetizers and watch a first-run film in luxury and comfort at the glamorous **Kabuki Sundance Cinema** in Japantown. Check out the art gallery, too.

Castro Theatre; 429 Castro Street; tel: 415-621-6120; map C3
The Roxie Film Center; 3117 16th Street; tel: 415-863-1087; map E4
Red Vic; 1727 Haight Street; tel: 415-668-3994; map A4
Kabuki Sundance Cinema; 1881 Post Street; tel: 415-346-3243; map D5

Immerse yourself in the heart of the Castro **gay scene** at **Café Flore**

San Francisco is often referred to as the gay capital of the world, a title its residents wear with pride. The active lesbian and gay community that has made its home in the Castro has contributed significantly to every area of San Francisco's culture: economic, artistic, and political.

Established in 1973, funky **Café Flore** has been the pulsing heart of the Castro, morning, noon, and night. A colorful and eclectic mix of gay, straight, buff, skinny, locals and travelers converge at the busy intersection of Market, Noe and 16th streets for strong coffee, boozy brunches, outdoor dining, nightly drink specials, mingling, and cruising. Order the decadent mac 'n' cheese or a shrimp and avocado salad, kick back, and enjoy the parade of phenomenal people-watching.

East on Market is another epicenter of gay culture – or rather, lesbian, gay, bisexual, and transgender culture. **The Center** opened at the height of the AIDS pandemic and celebrates the history, culture, and diversity of the community. There is a gallery and cafe on the premises of the modern, solar-powered, 35,000-sq-ft facility as well as community bulletin boards, free Internet, and

a general information desk with a wide gamut of resources for the LBGT community. It also offers support groups, youth programs, yoga classes, writing workshops, and even Weight Watchers and 12-step meetings.

Café Flore; 2298 Market Street; tel: 415-621-8579; http://cafeflore.com; Sun–Thur 7am–1am, Fri–Sat 7am–2am; map B4
The Center; 1800 Market Street; tel: 415-865-5555; Mon–Thur noon–10pm, Fri noon–6pm, Sat 9am–6pm; map E5

Outer Neighborhoods

Outer Neighborhoods

Marin Headlands
Golden Gate Bridge

Fort Point
National Historic Park

Warming Hut

San Francisco Bay

Golden Gate National Recreation Area

CRISSY FIELD

Exploratori

Senspa

Palace of Fine Arts

0   ½   1 mile
0   ½   1 km

PACIFIC OCEAN

Golden Gate National Recreation Area

PRESIDIO

PRESIDIO HEIGHTS

JULIUS KAHN PLAYGROUND

PRESIDIO GOLF COURSE

Arguello Gate

LAURE HEIGH

Eagle's Point

Palace of the Legion of Honor

Florence Gould Theatre

Land's End

LINCOLN PARK GOLF COURSE

LINCOLN PARK

Seal Rock Inn

Lake St

California St

Clement

Pizzetta 211

Gaspare's

Clement

CLEMENT STREET

See right

Pot de Pho

Geary

University of San Francisco

Sutro Baths

Cliff House

Anza St

RICHMOND

Geary Blvd

Balboa St

Cabrillo St

Fulton St

Fulton St

PANHAND

HAIGH ASHBU

de Young Museum

GOLDEN GATE PARK GOLF COURSE

GOLDEN GATE PARK

Kezar Dr

TWIN PEAK

Lincoln Way

Hotel

Naan n Curry

Java Beach Café

see below

Irving St

Judah St

Kirkham St

Lawton St

Moraga St

Noriega St

7th Ave

19th Ave

Noriega St

Ortega St

SUNSET

Pacheco St

Quintara St

FOREST HILL

Riviera St

Santiago St

Taraval St

Taraval St

Ulloa St

Taraval St

Vincente St

MOUNT DAVISON PARK

Ocean Park Motel

PINE LAKE PARK

Sloat Blvd

47th   46th   45th   44th   43rd

San Francisco Zoo

Other Avenues

Trouble Coffee

Judahlicious

Judah St

Judah St

General Store

Outerlands

Near Ocean Beach

Skyline Blvd

Lake Merced

LAKE MERCED PARK

HARDING PARK GOLF COURSE

San Francisco State University

INGLESIDE

152

A   B   C   D

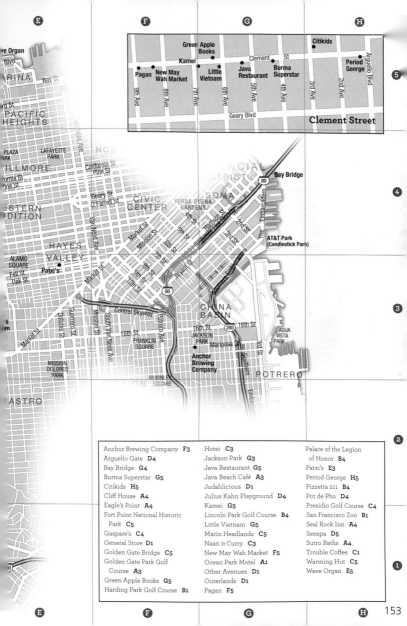

Clement Street

Get rejuvenated at a spa in a former army barracks after a Presidio run

Ironically, the world's largest urban national park is sometimes overlooked as a visitors' destination. A former army base, the 1,491-acre **Presidio** encompasses shoreline, coastal bluffs, wooded hilltops, and prairie grasslands, and is the location of filmmaker George Lucas's Digital Arts Center, restaurants and cafes, historic buildings, Baker Beach, 22 hiking trails, and two playgrounds.

Take the **Ecology Trail**, accessed through the Arguello Gate. It goes past the Inspiration Point overlook with panoramic bay views and the Presidio forest. A connecting trail brings you to **Julius Kahn**, the city's poshest playground, which will delight kids with its cool climbing structures. From there, connect to **Lovers' Lane**, first used by Spanish soldiers and Franciscan missionaries.

When your muscles get weary, it is time to head to the Presidio's spa. Located in a cavernous 13,000-sq-ft former army barracks, **Senspa** goes beyond the usual menu of massages, facials, and body treatments – you get the services of a 'master aromatherapist' and a wellness coach, plus body scrubs customized for your skin.

The Presidio; tel: 415-561-5418; www. presidio.gov; map D4
Senspa; 1161 Gorgas Avenue; tel: 415-441-1777; www.senspa.com; Tue–Fri 10am–9pm, Sat–Sun 9am–7pm; map D5

BURNING MAN

It would be remiss to write a book about San Francisco without mentioning **Burning Man**. The genesis of the annual Dionysian arts extravaganza that erupts in Black Rock Desert, Nevada, in early September was on the shores of the Presidio's Baker Beach. On the summer solstice of 1986, Larry Harvey burned a wooden man in effigy as part of a purification ritual. This act sparked what would evolve into an international art movement and experiment in cooperative off-the-grid living with upwards of 50,000 participants.

Stroll along the bay from Crissy Field to a haunted military fort

In a city of great walks, the 3½-mile **Golden Gate Promenade** that hugs the bay is truly spectacular. Begin at the Marina Green, a lush expanse of lawn in front of the St Francis Yacht Club and a prime kite-flying locale.

Well-toned runners, skaters, and cyclists whizz by, and there is often a volleyball game being played on the green. Turn on Yacht Road past the harbor and walk to the end of the narrow jetty to reach the **Wave Organ** (map E5). This acoustic sculpture of 25 pipes resonates to the motion of waves, making subtle sounds best heard at low tide.

On to **Crissy Field**. A 100-acre site that once housed a military airstrip was restored to an environmental wonderland, with a wetlands preserve, a tidal marsh, pocket beaches, grassy bluffs,

lagoons, and a habitat for herons, pelicans, and other native species.

Meander along and stop for hot chocolate and a bite at the cozy **Warming Hut**. The gift shop sells a selection of books and eco-friendly souvenirs like wallets made from recycled materials.

Once refreshed, press on to **Fort Point**, the formidable fortress below the Golden Gate Bridge, built at the onset of the Civil War. According to local lore, the fort is haunted. Those who are not easily spooked should take the candlelit tour, offered monthly in winter. Call 415-556-1693 for reservations.

Warming Hut; Marine Drive; tel: 415-561-3040; daily 9am–5pm; map C5
Fort Point; end of Marine Drive; tel: 415-561-4395; www.nps.gov/fopo; Fri–Sun 10am–5pm; free; map C5

Pedal a bike across the Golden Gate Bridge to the Marin Headlands or Sausalito

The magnificent **Golden Gate Bridge** is the city's most recognized and beloved icon, and certainly one of the most photographed bridges in the world. Finished in 1937, having cost $35 million, it stretches 1¾ miles from the northern edge of the Presidio to the southern tip of the Marin Headlands and is suspended 220ft above the mouth of the San Francisco Bay. The Golden Gate, painted not gold but 'international orange,' is an engineering marvel and a stunning example of Art Deco design. Bike (or walk) across and experience the grandeur up close.

Use sunscreen and dress appropriately in layers and a jacket – if the wind picks up or fog rolls in, the temperature can drop drastically. You can rent bicycles at many shops in the city, but **Blazing Saddles** in Fisherman's Wharf has easy access to the bike path that crosses the bridge, and bikes come equipped with maps. If you are planning to come back via the ferry *(below)*, you can also purchase tickets here.

Cyclists cross the bridge on the west side, pedestrians on the east. Feel the wind in your face and take in breathtaking views as you cross this splendid landmark. Once on the Marin side, you can choose to veer left on Conzelman Road to the Headlands, or cross beneath the freeway toward Sausalito. Cycling through the wild, majestic beauty of the **Marin Headlands**, where rolling green hills give way to craggy cliffs that plunge down to the Pacific, is well worth the effort, but should only be attempted by experienced and fit cyclists.

Otherwise coast downhill to Sausalito or Tiburon. Stop for ice cream at **Lappert's** (689 Bridgeway) in the chic but sweet **Sausalito**, lock your bike and poke around the shops and galleries. If you choose to stay for lunch, **The Spinnaker** has good seafood and unrivaled views of the waterfront. From here, press on for nine pleasant coastal miles along Richardson Bay. Your reward is delightful downtown **Tiburon** and lunch harborside on the sunny back patio of **Sam's Anchor Café**.

From either town, you can pedal back to the bridge or board a ferry back to the city (with your bike). Be advised – it is a steep ride back to the bridge from Sausalito. The ferry option is the way to go for most, but be sure to check the ferry schedule.

Blazing Saddles; 2715 Hyde Street; tel: 415-202-8888; daily 8am–8pm; map p.24 C4
The Spinnaker; 100 Spinnaker Drive, Sausalito; tel: 415-332-1500; www.the spinnaker.com; daily Br, L, & D
Sam's Anchor Café; 27 Main Street, Tiburon; tel: 415-435-4527; www.sams cafe.com; daily Br, L, & D

Bargain-hunt in shops on **Clement Street** and browse **Green Apple Books**

Clement Street is referred to by many as San Francisco's 'other Chinatown.' But while there is a significant Chinese population here, many other cultures converge to make up its vibrant tapestry. You'll find Russian groceries, Irish bars, a German bakery, and a Turkish-owned gourmet food store. Among the proliferation of 'dollar stores,' brimming with cheap plastic goods, you can find some retail gems.

Start near Sixth Avenue and pop into **New May Wah Market** (547 Clement Street; tel: 415-668-2583) for a culture experience and culinary primer. Marvel not only at the vast selection of exotic produce and Chinese specialty foods, but also the prices.

On the corner, **Kamei** (no. 525–547; tel: 415-666-3688) is stocked floor-to-ceiling with ceramic bowls, Asian dinnerware, pretty serving trays, teapots, and kitchen gadgets. Boxed sets of Japanese bowls make nice gifts, and prices are beyond reasonable.

Across the street is one of the city's great independent bookstores. It is easy to lose a few hours at ramshackle **Green Apple Books** (no. 506; tel: 415-387-2272), browsing new and used books in the rambling space with multiple levels and a huge selection of children's books.

From sippy cups and slings to car seats and clothes, anything you need for babies can be found at **Citikids** (no. 152; tel: 415-752-3837). At the end of Clement, **Period George** (no. 7; tel: 415-752-1900) is lavish and lovely, filled with a pretty mix of found objects, museum-quality *objets d'art*, and kitsch.

Clement Street; map F5–H5

Decide on the Richmond's **best thin-crust pizza** – Pizetta 211 or Gaspare's

San Francisco embraces pizza in all of its saucy splendor. While the Richmond district is best known for fog, ethnic restaurants, and access to Golden Gate Park, two highly contrasting experiences of thin-crust pizza await your taste buds.

Cozy, charming **Pizzetta 211** has just four tables inside, plus a few out front beneath strings of white lights. With the exception of some standing items, the menu changes weekly, based on what is seasonally available. Your topping might be shiitake

mushrooms with house-cured pancetta and pecorino cheese, or the simple perfection of the Margherita – tomato, mozarella, and basil. They also offer inventive salads and calzone.

A few blocks away, beneath a trellis of dusty Chianti bottles and plastic grapes, sink into a booth at homey, family-friendly **Gaspare's**. Put a quarter into the tableside jukebox and select tunes from an era when the Beach Boys were Top 40. The menu is large – pastas, classic Italian entrees, and salads – but do yourself a favor, order the pizza alla Napoletana and be prepared for thin-crust pizza mastery. Fold it in half lengthwise and enjoy.

Of course, you can enjoy pizza perfection all over town – from pillowy Sicilian squares à la **Golden Boy** (542 Green Street; tel: 415-982-9738) to beautifully blistered Neapolitan pies at **Delfina** (3611 18th Street; tel: 415-437-6800) to deep-dish delights at **Patxi's** (511 Hayes Street; tel: 415-558-9991).

Pizzetta 211; 211 23rd Avenue; tel: 415-379-9880; map B4
Gaspare's; 5546 Geary Boulevard; tel: 415-387-5025; map C4

Ramble along the coast, then celebrate with champagne at the **Cliff House**

The city's most dramatic hiking trail winds along wild, craggy coastline, where the sea crashes violently against cliffs at the edge of the continent. It is unfathomably gorgeous, and appropriately named **Land's End**.

Start at the **Sutro Baths** (map A4). What you see is all that is left of this early resort, which opened in 1897 with seven megapools of varying temperatures, then fell into disuse and burned in 1966.

Find the Coastal Trail sign at the top of the parking lot, above the ruins. Enter beneath a canopy of twisted cypress trees, eerily carved by the wind. The waters below are strewn with the wrecks of ships that failed to navigate this dangerous curve and sank to their watery graves. Look for the rusted remains of *Lyman Stewart* and *Frank Buck* at low tide near **Mile Rock Beach**.

Continue savoring magnificent views along the 1½-mile clifftop trail to **Eagle's Point** (map A4), or venture down footpaths to discover secret coves, pocket beaches, and a hidden labyrinth. Use caution – the cliff paths are steep and without guardrails.

When you have had your fill of coastal loveliness, head back toward the Sutro Baths. All that clambering merits a bottle of bubbly. Luckily the handsome, historic **Cliff House** is poised on a nearby bluff. Settle into a window seat, at either the **Bistro** or the fancier, pricier **Sutro's**, and pop the cork.

The Cliff House; 1090 Point Lobos Avenue; tel: 415-386-3330; www.cliff house.com; daily L & D, Sun Br; Sutro's: approx $55 per person, three courses, no wine; Bistro: approx $45 per person, three courses, no wine; map A4

Tee off at one of the city's scenic **golf courses**

Golfers will be pleased to note that San Francisco has a few great options to get you out on the green without leaving the city.

Just east of the Palace of the Legion of Honor *(p.162)*, the **Lincoln Park Golf Course** is a hilly but walkable 18-hole course. The fairways are lined with cypresses, and you can catch glimpses of the Golden Gate Bridge, the city, and the ocean along the course.

Open from sunrise to sundown, the 9-hole, par-27 **Golden Gate Park Golf Course** is casual, fun, and inexpensive. The course hosts tournaments, has a practice range, and offers junior and adult instructions through Beyond the Ball Golf School. Enjoy a meat feast at the on-site Ironwood BBQ.

The 18-hole, par-72 **Presidio Golf Course and Clubhouse** has a practice center and professional instructors to help improve your game. The challenging course winds through fragrant eucalyptus trees and Monterey pines.

According to locals, the gorgeous 18-hole **Harding Park Golf Course** is the crème de la crème. The course has undergone an $18 million refurbishment and is the only one to feature a 25-tee driving range.

Lincoln Park Golf Course; 300 34th Avenue; tel: 415-221-9911; map B4
Golden Gate Park Golf Course; 47th Avenue at Fulton Street; tel: 415-751-8987; map A3
Presidio Golf Course and Clubhouse; 300 Finley Road at Arguello Gate; tel: 415-561-4661; map C4
Harding Park Golf Course; 99 Harding Road; tel: 415-664-4690; map B1

Contemplate life with Rodin's *The Thinker* at the Legion of Honor

From its perch above the city in tranquil Lincoln Park, the lovely **Palace of the Legion of Honor** overlooks the Pacific Ocean and the Golden Gate Bridge. This French neoclassical gem houses a collection spanning 4,000 years of ancient and European art in an exquisite setting.

Step into the domed rotunda and explore the Legion's treasures, which include European decorative arts and paintings, ancient art, and one of the largest collections of prints and drawings in the country. European paintings include masterworks from the 14th–20th centuries. Lose yourself in the visions of Picasso, Matisse, Rubens, Rembrandt, Monet, and El Greco.

Outside, among the formal gardens, colonnades, and fountains, is an imposing bronze sculpture sitting in pensive rumination. *The Thinker* is considered by many to be Auguste Rodin's best-known monumental work. The piece was originally conceived in 1880 as the poet Dante, but evolved over time to become a representation of all poets and artists. *The Thinker* is one of the earliest acquisitions of more than 70 Rodin sculptures donated to the museum.

Don't leave the museum grounds without contemplating the grim yet powerful Holocaust Memorial by George Segal, a contemporary of Warhol and Lichtenstein in the Pop Art movement. The haunting memorial is northeast of the museum overlooking Land's End.

The museum offers free Saturday family tours and hands-on art projects led by professional artists. Weekend visitors are treated to public organ concerts on Saturday and Sunday at 4pm.

Palace of the Legion of Honor; 100 34th Avenue; tel: 415-750-3600; www.famsf. org; Tue–Sun 9.30am–5pm; charge; map B4

Listen to English translations of **opera classics** at the **Florence Gould Theatre**

Pocket Opera is the brainchild of pianist Donald Pippin, who in 1954 was performing in small chamber ensembles in North Beach cabarets. The performances evolved into vocal recitals and one-act operas that became hugely popular. Pippin felt strongly that opera should be accessible to a wider audience, and began transcribing operas into English.

Fast-forward 25 years – the company had grown out of cabarets and into theaters. Since then, Pocket Opera has performed an annual season with an expanding repertory of operas, from familiar classics to forgotten gems. Pippin has changed the way audiences see, hear, and understand opera, making it an accessible form of musical theater.

Pocket Opera productions are minimally staged, use basic costumes, and only props that are essential to the story. Some are performed concert-style. Past performances include *La Vie Parisienne, Cinderella, La Rondine,* and *La Traviata.*

San Francisco Pocket Opera productions are performed at the intimate **Florence Gould Theatre** in the **Palace of the Legion of Honor.** The 316-seat jewel-box theater, decorated in the Louis XVI style with an elaborate Spanish mural on the ceiling, has hosted diverse artists, from Joan Baez and Andrés Segovia to Marcel Marceau and Duke Ellington.

Pocket Opera; Florence Gould Theatre, Palace of the Legion of Honor, 100 34th Avenue; tel: 415-972-8930; www. pocketopera.org; season runs Feb–July, check website for schedule; map B4

OPERA IN THE PARK
Opera in the Park is a free annual concert that takes place every September at Sharon Meadow in Golden Gate Park. Members of the San Francisco Opera perform arias and operatic excerpts, accompanied by the San Francisco Opera Orchestra.

Hang out with surfers at Java Beach Café near Ocean Beach

The cool, windswept outer Sunset has a distinctive character. With the powerful Pacific as its backdrop, it retains a hippie, groovy beach-town feel, though a pervasive chill keeps less hardy folks away. Surfers brave the waves and cyclists, skaters, and runners hit the paved esplanade that stretches for miles along the Great Highway. Colorful kites soar above the dunes year-round. And on rare hot days, Ocean Beach is a paradise.

Laidback **Java Beach Café** (1396 La Playa Street; tel: 415-665-5282;

map A3) is a haven for locals, surfers, beach bums, and writers. It is the perfect place to sip a pint outside on a sunny afternoon, or hole yourself up with a latte and a bowl of soup in foggy weather.

A few blocks east, **Other Avenues** (3930 Judah Street; tel: 415-661-7475; map D1) is a vegetarian grocery with organic produce and bulk foods. The funky orange spot on the corner is **Judahlicious** (3906 Judah Street; tel: 415-665-8423; map D1), a raw food, vegan, and juice bar for your hemp milk smoothie needs.

Some pockets of greatness have emerged on the next block. Quirky **Trouble Coffee** (4033 Judah Street; tel: 415-682-4732; map C1) is a pocket-size joint offering stellar coffee drinks, fresh coconuts with straws, slabs of cinnamon toast, and unusual banter. The carefully curated **General Store** (4035 Judah Street; tel: 415-682-0600; map D1) has an eclectic assortment of things you will desperately want to buy. And dragging the neighborhood to the culinary playing field, **Outerlands** (4001 Judah Street; tel: 415-661-6140; map D1) is rustic gem serving outstanding simple, homey, and thoughtfully prepared food in a beach-and-driftwood ambience.

Expand your **global culinary palate** at one of many **ethnic eateries**

The Sunset and the Richmond are two mostly flat neighborhoods that run parallel to Golden Gate Park. While largely residential areas, they are also known for a dazzling array of ethnic foods, from Thai to Taiwanese, Indian to Indonesian, with Burmese, Japanese, French, Italian, Vietnamese, Chinese, Moroccan, Mexican, Middle Eastern, Russian, Korean, and Eritrean mixed in.

If you have never tried Burmese food, now is the time. The inner Richmond boasts at least four restaurants serving this flavorful, distinct cuisine, informed by Thai, Chinese, and Indian flavors yet completely unique. Two popular choices are **Burma Superstar** (309 Clement Street; tel: 415-387-2147; map G5) and **Pagan** (3199 Clement Street; tel: 415-751-2598; map F5) – order the tea-leaf or rainbow salad and samosa soup.

For Vietnamese, **Pot de Pho** (3300 Geary Boulevard; tel: 415-668-0826; map D4) make their own noodles and use fresh organic vegetables. The caramelized cast-iron catfish is sensational. **Little Vietnam** (309 Sixth Avenue; tel: 415-876-0283; map G5) falls into the bargain-bites category, with counter seating, imperial rolls over noodles, papaya salad, noodle soups, and rice plates. The truly budget-conscious can fill up on a plate of super-cheap peanut noodles with a side of kimchi at **Java Restaurant** (417 Clement Street; tel: 415-752-1541; map G5).

Over in the Sunset, **Naan n Curry** (642 Irving Street; tel: 415-664-7225; map C3) is a consistently tasty, inexpensive option for no-frills Indian. Don't leave town without sampling their tikka masala. For gyoza, generous noodle bowls, and excellent sushi in a classy, relaxing atmosphere, check out **Hotei** (1290 9th Avenue; tel: 415-753-6045; map C3).

Take a walk through an **African Savanna** at the **San Francisco Zoo**

Contemporary zoos pride themselves on being humane wildlife sanctuaries that promote education and interaction – and this is certainly the case at **San Francisco Zoo**.

Over the years, the zoo has embraced the trend of moving animals from individual cages into well-designed, landscaped habitats. A wonderful example of this is the **African Savanna**. As you enter the zoo, turn right and look for the elegant silhouettes of giraffes in the distance. They roam in a 3-acre multi-species habitat that includes zebra, kudu, and horned oryx, with a winding boardwalk allowing visitors to get close.

A perennial favorite exhibit is the **Lemur Forest**, where an elevated ramp a llows you to watch the shenanigans of these adorable primates as they swing and climb. Close by, **Penguin Island** is the most successful breeding colony of Magellanic penguins in the world. Check

the feeding schedule so you're sure to catch the charismatic aquatic birds being hand-fed.

It is always a thrill to visit the **Lion House** and the outdoor habitat where the majestic big cats roam. Watch as fierce, beautiful lions and tigers lumber about and let out bone-chilling roars.

Farther afield is **Grizzly Gulch**, where bears Kachina and Kiona are fed daily at 11am. Stop by and see these awesome creatures romp, forage and chow down.

San Francisco Zoo; 1 Zoo Road; tel: 415-753-7080; www.sfzoo.org; daily, mid-Mar–early Nov 10am–5pm, early Nov–mid-Mar 10am–4pm; charge; map B1

Sample San Francisco's famous **steam beer** on a **brewery tour**

The dark amber liquid you might have noticed flowing from taps, or being guzzled from yellow-labeled bottles all over town, is San Francisco's prized brew, Anchor Steam.

The roots of the **Anchor Brewing Company** go back to the Gold Rush, when German brewer Gottlieb Brekle arrived in 1854 and opened a brewery on Pacific Avenue. It changed hands over the years and eventually became known as Anchor, a nod to the Barbary Coast.

Today, Anchor Steam beers are crafted in a gleaming copper brewhouse, one of the most traditional in the world. Anchor offers free two-hour walking tours of the facility that include a history of the brewery and culminate in a sample tasting session of a selection of their eight brews. Tours are quite popular and available by phone reservation only, so plan ahead as they book up – call during business hours (9am–5pm). Children are welcome on the tour, but bring juice boxes – sorry, no tastings for the kiddies.

Insider tip: if you don't have reservations, call a day or two before and ask about cancellations.

Anchor Brewing Company; 1705 Mariposa Street; tel: 415-863-8350; www. anchorbrewing.com; free; map F3

hotels

From five-star splendor to quirky boutique hotels to cheap sleeps, San Francisco offers travelers no shortage of unique and memorable places to stay. Hotel groups that specialize in creative niche properties include Joie de Vivre, Personality, and Kimpton, often offering complimentary evening wine, breakfast, in-room coffee, and free Wi-Fi. Be sure to ask about Internet and parking charges when booking, as many established hotels charge ridiculously high fees.

Most of the city's hotels are clustered around Union Square and, more recently, SoMa. Though both are busy, congested areas, the advantage is their proximity to some of the great museums, restaurants, and shopping, as well as good public transportation.

Fisherman's Wharf accommodations tend to be bland, while Nob Hill is home to the grand palaces of distinction like the Fairmont. And though a highly desirable location, there are relatively few places to stay in North Beach.

A room in Haight-Ashbury is ideal for those seeking nightlife, access to Golden Gate Park, and an authentic glimpse into the city. Regal, residential Pacific Heights is sedate, with unparalleled views. Options close to the ocean tend to be motor lodges and motels, and Lombard Street in the Marina is also known for its strip of inexpensive motels.

HOTEL PRICES
A standard room in peak season:

$$$$ over $300
$$$ $180–300
$$ $100–180
$ under $100

Family-Friendly

Argonaut Hotel
Fisherman's Wharf
495 Jefferson Street; tel: 415-563-0800;
www.argonauthotel.com; map p.24 C4; $$$
Children are greeted with gifts, pets
are warmly welcomed, and the evening
wine hour in the chic lobby is casual
and friendly. The Wharf's best hotel is
tricked out in nautical style, in keeping
with the Hyde Street Pier location. The
Blue Mermaid restaurant has a tasty
selection of chowder, seafood dishes,
and comfort food.

Hotel Union Square
Union Square
114 Powell Street; tel: 415-397-3000; www.
hotelunionsquare.com; map p.62 D2; $$$
A dedicated children's suite is
loaded with items to keep youngsters
occupied – from toddler toys to a Wii.
Literary types should note Dashiell
Hammett booked his fiancée a room
here the night before their wedding.
An eponymous suite is decorated with
Hammett ephemera.

Hotel Metropolis
Union Square
25 Mason Street; tel: 415-775-4600; www.
hotelmetropolis.com; map p.62 C2; $$$
The kids' suite is whimsical and fun,
comprised of three connecting rooms,
one with a bunk bed. A sitting room
with refrigerator, microwave, writing
desks, computer, and television makes
for a comfortable stay.

Money No Object

Four Seasons Hotel
SoMa

757 Market Street; tel: 415-633-3000; www.fourseasons.com/sanfrancisco; map p.79 E3; $$$$

This is where The Rolling Stones and Jerry Seinfeld stay when they're in town. True to the brand, the Four Seasons offers understated luxury and impeccable service. Bathrooms with deep tubs are swathed in marble, and views from the modern glass high-rise are exquisite. What's not to love?

The Ritz-Carlton
Nob Hill/Financial District

600 Stockton Street; tel: 415-296-7465; www.ritzcarlton.com; map p.44 D5; $$$–$$$$

A recent $12.5 million renovation secured this hotel a position among the world's best. Lavish guest rooms feature original work by local artists, 400-thread-count linens, high-def flat-screen televisions, iPod docking stations, and double sinks in bathrooms. The Dining Room restaurant is one of the city's best.

St Regis Hotel
SoMa

125 Third Street; tel: 415-296-7465; www.stregis.com/sanfrancisco; map p.79 E3; $$$$

Luxury meets technology meets art in a beautiful historic building with an attached, modern 40-story tower. Your personal butler escorts you to your room and demonstrates the touch-screen panel that controls everything from drapes to television to thermostat. Get your art fix next door at SFMOMA.

Rooms with a View

Sir Francis Drake
🟦 **Union Square**
450 Powell Street; tel: 415-392-7755; www.
sirfrancisdrake.com; map p.62 D3; $$$
Enjoy the stellar panoramic views
from Harry Denton's Starlight Room
at the top, where you can also dance,
drink, and listen to live music. Scala's
Bistro on the street level offers
traditional Italian with a modern twist.

The Westin St Francis
🟦 **Union Square**
335 Powell Street; tel: 415-397-7000; www.
westinstfrancis.com; map p.62 C3; $$$
The city's original world-class hotel
overlooks Union Square with majestic
splendor. The fashionable Clock
Bar and acclaimed Michael Mina
restaurant are opposite in the lobby.
Rooms in the old building have more
character, but the trip to the tower in
glass elevators showcases mind-
blowing views.

InterContinental San Francisco
🟦 **SoMa**
888 Howard Street; tel: 415-616-6500; www.
intercontinentalsanfrancisco.com; map p.79
E2; $$–$$$$
A James Bond assignment in San
Francisco might find him ensconced
here. Tall, sexy, and technologically
sophisticated, this 32-story hotel is
befitting of a special agent. 007 might
even switch from the miniature vodka
Martini after sampling one of the
grappas from Bar 888's collection.

Historic Hotels

The Huntington Hotel
■ Nob Hill
1075 California Street; tel: 415-474-5400;
www.huntingtonhotel.com; map p.44 C5; $$$$

This storied hotel captures the refinement of old money. Family-owned since 1924, publicity-shy celebrities and dignitaries stay here in discreet luxury and enjoy old-world service. Opulent suites have been featured in *Architectural Digest*, and the Nob Hill Spa on the premises is the city's best.

Palace Hotel
■ Financial District
2 New Montgomery Street; tel: 415-512-1111; www.sfpalace.com; map p.63 E3; $$$

Built in 1875, the Palace still retains a 'wow' factor. The magnificent Garden Court ceiling is made of 80,000 panes of stained glass. Maxfield Parish painted the 16ft mural displayed in the Pied Piper bar. Among the impressive list of guests are a series of American presidents, Oscar Wilde, Sarah Bernhardt, and Enrico Caruso.

The Fairmont
■ Nob Hill
950 Mason Street; tel: 415-772-5000; www.fairmont.com/sanfrancisco; map p.44 C5; $$$

The grande dame of San Francisco hotels was set to open the day of the 1906 earthquake. Architect Juila Morgan restored it and one year later it debuted. The glittering marble lobby stuns with Corinthian columns, a grand staircase, and plush furnishings. Rooms have extra-long mattresses, Frette linens, and goose-down pillows.

dget Beds

The Red Victorian

Haight-Ashbury
1665 Haight Street; tel: 415-864-1978; http://redvic.net; map p.114 B1; $–$$
Janis Joplin and Jerry Garcia have long since passed, but the Summer of Love is alive and well in this funky inn with colorful themed rooms. Some rooms share baths, and breakfast at the street-level Peace Café is included.

San Remo Hotel
North Beach
2237 Mason Street; tel: 415-776-868; map p.24 D3; $
This Euro-style pension is a slice of maritime and bohemian history. The Italianate Victorian provided refuge to sailors, poets, and artists and now features lovingly restored details like stained-glass skylights, carved fretwork, and redwood wainscoting. Hallway nooks are perfect for reading, and shared bathrooms are impeccable.

Fisherman's Wharf Hostel
Marina
Building 240, Fort Mason; tel: 415-771-7277; www.sfhostels.com; map p.96 D1; $
This hostel is a hidden gem in a prime location overlooking the bay at Fort Mason. Dorm rooms with bunks are super cheap, but for a bit more you can reserve a stark, functional private room. Parking is free, and breakfast at organic Café Franco, with views of Alcatraz and the Golden Gate Bridge, is included.

Away from it All

Hotel Drisco
■ **Pacific Heights**
2901 Pacific Avenue; tel: 415-346-2880;
www.jdvhotels.com/drisco; map p.97 B4;
$$–$$$

This classy hotel befits the city's
most affluent neighborhood. From
a civilized wine hour to the gourmet
breakfast spread, the Drisco makes you
feel like you are staying with wealthy
relations, in your own private wing.

Seal Rock Inn
■ **Land's End/Outer Richmond**
545 Point Lobos Avenue; tel: 415-752-8000;
www.sealrockinn.com; map p.152 A4; $$

In a wonderful location near Land's
End, far from the downtown bustle,
this motor lodge offers free parking
and lovely ocean views. Some rooms
are dated and dowdy, but others have
kitchenettes, and spacious top-floor
rooms have fireplaces.

Ocean Park Motel
■ **Outer Sunset**
2690 46th Avenue; tel: 415-566-7020; www.
oceanparkmotel.com; map p.152 A1; $$

A few blocks from the zoo and Ocean
Beach, this Art Deco gem is impeccably
maintained and manicured. Some
rooms are tiny, but eight of the suites
have fully equipped kitchens, and an
outdoor hot tub is available to stave off
the Outer Sunset chill.

Affordable Style

Hotel Kabuki
Japantown
1625 Post Street; tel: 415-922-3200; www.
jdvhotels.com/kabuki; map p.97 D5; $$
Harmoniously blending Eastern
and Western influences in the heart
of Japantown, Hotel Kabuki offers
access to Japanese baths on the next
block, a tranquil Zen garden and the
O Izakaya Lounge. Japanese suites
with futons are great for families.

Hotel Palomar
SoMa
12 Fourth Street; tel: 415-348-1111; www.
hotelpalomar-sf.com; map p.78 D3; $$$
Rooms have spicy, colorful accents,
and the Palomar's art theme is
prevalent throughout. The world-
class Fifth Floor restaurant is within.
Details, amenities, and service are
exemplary in this whimsically stylish,
modern hotel. Stop by for the wine
hour and/or complimentary scoops of
ice cream.

Hotel Bohème
■ North Beach

444 Columbus Avenue; tel: 415-433-9111;
www.hotelboheme.com; map p.24 D1; $$$

This petite hotel is a shrine to the
Beat Generation, with gorgeous black-
and-white photographs and collages.
Bohème is softly lit, with walls painted
deep terracotta and windows heavily
draped. Sherry is served in the
afternoon. The best *cannoli* in town is
downstairs at Stella Pastry.

Hotel Rex
■ Union Square

562 Sutter Street; tel: 415-433-4434; www.
jdvhotels.com/rex; map p.62 C3; $$$

Inspired by the salons of the 1920s
and 1930s, this handsome hotel honors
literary legends in the same manner
as the Algonquin in New York. You
might stumble upon a poetry-reading
in the clubby book-lined lobby, or live
jazz at the library bar.

The Stanyan Park Hotel
■ Haight-Ashbury

750 Stanyan Street; tel: 415-751-1000;
www.stanyanpark.com; map p.114 A1; $$

Pretend it is your pied-à-terre in the
funky-chic Haight when you stay at
one of the apartment-style suites.
Single rooms are also delightful,
with built-in cabinetry, Victorian
furnishings, and lace curtains, many
flooded with light. Afternoon tea and
a breakfast buffet are served in an
elegant street-level parlor.

omantic Rendezvous

Washington Square Inn

North Beach

1660 Stockton Street; tel: 415-981-4220;
www.wsisf.com; map p.24 C2; $$$

Rooms are above Washington Square
in the city's romance-inducing Italian
neighborhood. After strolling the
hills, evening wine, hors d'oeuvres,
and a comfy pillow-top mattress
await. Elegant rooms mix modern and
Baroque touches.

Hotel Monaco
Union Square

501 Geary Street; tel: 415-292-0100; www.
monaco-sf.com; map p.62 C3; $$$

Indulge yourself and your paramour
at this glamorous boutique hotel.
French architecture and sensual
decor are augmented by evening
wine, cheese-tastings, and neck and
shoulder massages. The Grand Café, a
former ballroom, evokes the zinc bars
of 1920s Paris.

Hotel Majestic
Pacific Heights

1500 Sutter Street; tel: 415-441-1100; www.
thehotelmajestic.com; map p.96 E5; $$

Clawfoot bathtubs, French and
English antiques, and charming
sitting areas are hallmarks of this
gracious Edwardian hotel, a respite
from the downtown frenzy. Café
Majestic is critically acclaimed, and
the classy Butterfly Bar recalls old-
world San Francisco.

White Swan Inn
Union Square

845 Bush Street; tel: 415-775-1755; www.
jdvhotels.com/white_swan_inn; map p.62
C3; $$$

Dark wood, cozy nooks, and in-room
fireplaces create an intimate vibe.
Gourmet breakfasts are served near
a pocketsize garden, while evening
sherry, wine, and pastries are enjoyed
fireside in the parlor.

Hipster Hotels

Hotel Triton
🟦 **Union Square**
342 Grant Avenue; tel: 415-394-0500; www.
hoteltriton.com; map p.62 D3; $$$
Designer suites are named for
musicians, and the lobby features a
mural by I. M. Pei's daughter-in-law,
Kari Pei. A green sensibility prevails,
with eco-friendly products and natural
linens. Evening wine, tarot readings,
and chair massages are offered.
An international crowd hangs out
downstairs at Café de la Presse.

Hotel des Arts
🟦 **Union Square**
447 Bush Street; tel: 415-956-3232; www.sf
hoteldesarts.com; map p.63 E3; $–$$
Modest rooms are enhanced with
edgy art – each room is a canvas for
a different artist's vision. The lobby
doubles as a gallery for emerging
talent. Peruse the website to select a
room that suits your taste, then call to
book it.

The Phoenix Hotel
🟦 **Tenderloin**
601 Eddy Street; tel: 415-776-1380; www.
thephoenixhotel.com; map p.78 B3; $$
In a seedy neighborhood, hotelier
Joie de Vivre created an artsy oasis
with palm trees, sculpture garden,
and heated pool. Those who have
graced the sheets here include the Red
Hot Chili Peppers, the Killers, Franz
Ferdinand, David Bowie, and Pearl Jam.
Upping hipster cred is the Bambuddah
Lounge that spills into the pool area.

Essentials

A

Age Restrictions

You must be over 21 years of age to be able to drink legally in San Francisco. Expect to show ID to buy alcohol in bars, clubs, and restaurants.

C

Children

San Francisco is very kid-friendly, with an abundance of playgrounds, restaurants that offer children's menus, bathrooms equipped with changing tables for babies, and lots of open space. Most hotels allow children to stay in parents' rooms at no additional charge.

Good Internet resources for family travel include www.familytravelforum.com, www.familytravelnetwork.com, www.travelwithyourkids.com, and www.deliciousbaby.com.

Climate

San Francisco weather can change significantly from hour to hour and between neighborhoods. Spring is warm and sunny (average high in April 63°F/17°C; low 50°F/10°C), while summers can be overcast and typified by fog (average high in July 66°F/19°C; low 54°F/12°C). Come September and October, the summer chill is replaced with beautifully mild, sunny days (average high in September 70°F/21°C; low 56°F/14°C).

Rainstorms (no snow) appear in December and January (average high in January 56°F/14°C; low 46°F/8°C).

Clothing

Plan for variable weather and bring clothes that can be layered, as well as comfortable walking shoes. A raincoat and umbrella are vital for rainy winter months. The city's casual vibe means jeans, T-shirts, and tennis shoes are ubiquitous on streets and in many restaurants and entertainment venues. However, fancier eateries and nightclubs warrant something smarter.

Crime and Safety

Travelers should exercise common sense, avoiding seedy neighborhoods and being cautious about walking around alone and at night. Avoid parks after dark. Neighborhoods with less safe reputations include the Tenderloin, Civic Center, Western Addition, the Lower Haight, the Mission south of 24th Street, South of Market above 5th Street, and the Bayview district.

Customs

Adult visitors staying longer than 72 hours may bring the following into the country duty-free: 1 liter of wine or liquor; 100 cigars (non-Cuban), or 3lbs of tobacco, or 200 cigarettes; and gifts valued under $100.

No food (even in cans) or plants are permissible. Visitors may also arrive and depart with up to $10,000 currency without needing to declare it. For the most up-to-date information, refer to the US Customs and Border Protection website (www.cbp.gov).

D

Disabled Travelers

The city's topography presents challenges to those who have mobility problems, but San Francisco is relatively 'disabled-friendly.'

Societies that can provide useful information include MossRehab (tel: 800-2255-6677; www.mossresourcenet. org) and the Society for Accessible Travel & Hospitality (SATH; tel: 212-447-7284; www.sath.org).

E

Electricity

Electricity in the US is 110 Volts, 60 Hertz AC. Flat-blade, two-pronged plugs are typical, though some points have three-pronged sockets. Most foreign appliances need a transformer and/or plug adapter.

Embassies and Consulates

Australia: tel: 536-1970; www.dfat. gov.au.
Canada: tel: 834-3180; www. sanfrancisco.gc.ca.
Ireland: tel: 392-4214; www. irelandemb.org.

New Zealand: tel: 399-1255; www. nzembassy.com/usa.
South Africa: tel: 202-232-4400; www. saembassy.org.
UK: tel: 617-1300; www.britainusa. com/sf.
Details for other embassies and consulates can be found in the Yellow Pages.

Emergency Numbers

For ambulance, fire, or police, dial 911; if you need to call from a public phone, no coins are needed.

F

Festivals

Check www.onlyinsanfrancisco.com/ calendar for festival and events listings.

G

Gay Travelers

San Francisco is internationally known as one of the world's most welcoming places for gays and lesbians. The most predominantly gay district is the Castro. The best sources for information are two free weeklies: the *Bay Area Reporter* (www.ebar. com) and the *Bay Area Times* (www. sfbaytimes.com). Also consult www. onlyinsanfrancisco.com/gaytravel. The Center (1800 Market Street; tel: 865-5555; www.sfcenter.org) is a nexus for the LGBT community, and has an information desk, library, web access, bulletin boards, and cafe.

H
Health
Drugstores (Pharmacies)
Some medicines that are available over the counter at home may require a prescription in the US. Branches of 24-hour Walgreens drugstore include: 498 Castro Street, tel: 861-3136; 1189 Potrero Avenue, tel: 647-1397; 3201 Divisadero Street, tel: 931-6417.

Additional Walgreens branches are open late.

Insurance and Hospitals
Healthcare is private and can be very expensive, especially if you need to be hospitalized. Foreign visitors should always ensure that they have full medical insurance covering their stay before traveling to the US. The following hospitals have 24-hour emergency rooms:

California Pacific Medical Center
Castro Street at Duboce Avenue; tel: 415-600-6000; www.cpmc.org.

Saint Francis Memorial Hospital
900 Hyde Street; tel: 353-6300; www.saintfrancismemorial.org.

San Francisco General Hospital
1001 Potrero Avenue; tel: 206-8000; www.sfdph.org.

UCSF Medical Center
505 Parnassus Avenue; tel: 476-1000; www.ucsfhealth.org.

I
Internet
Many cafes and some hotels have free or inexpensive Wi-Fi, and public library branches provide free web access (San Francisco Public Library; tel: 557-4400; http://sfpl.org).

M
Media
The largest regional newspaper is the *San Francisco Chronicle* (www.sfgate.com); its Sunday 'Pink Pages' list art, music, and entertainment events. Free alternative weeklies are found in newspaper boxes, cafes, and bars. The main weeklies are the *San Francisco Bay Guardian* (www.sfbg.com), *SF Weekly* (www.sfweekly.com), *San Francisco Bay Times* (www.sfbaytimes.com), and *Bay Area Reporter* (www.ebar.com). The last two are gay- and lesbian-oriented and easily found in the Castro. Online guides include www.sfstation.com, Laughing Squid (http://squidlist.com/events), Flavorpill (http://sf.flavorpill.net), MetroWize (www.metrowize.com), and Nitevibe (www.nitevibe.com). Two city magazines are *San Francisco* (www.sanfranmag.com) and *7x7* (www.7x7.com).

Money
Currency
The dollar ($) is divided into 100 cents (¢). Common coins are the penny (1¢),

nickel (5¢), dime (10¢), and quarter (25¢). Common bills are the $1, $5, $10, $20, $50, and $100 bills.

Banks and Currency Exchange
Bank hours are generally Monday to Friday, from about 9am to 5pm. Some open on Saturdays. It's best to change foreign currency at airports and major banks downtown.

ATMs
ATMs are at banks, some stores and bars, and charge varying usage fees: check also with your bank at home.

Traveller's Checks
Banks, stores, restaurants, and hotels generally accept traveller's checks in US dollars.

P
Police
The emergency police number is 911 (no coins needed). The non-emergency number for the police is 553-0123.

Postal Services
Post offices open at 8–9am and close at 5–6pm, Monday through Friday; the post office in the Macy's department store on Union Square (tel: 956-0131) is also open on Saturday and Sunday.
US Postal Service: tel: 800-275-8777; www.usps.com.

Public Holidays
National holidays are: New Year's Day (Jan 1); Martin Luther King Jr Day (3rd Mon in Jan); President's Day (3rd Mon in Feb); Memorial Day (Last Mon in May); Independence Day (July 4); Labor Day (1st Mon in Sept); Columbus Day (2nd Mon in Oct); Veterans Day (Nov 11); Thanksgiving Day (4th Thur in Nov); and Christmas (Dec 25).

S
Smoking
Smoking laws are strict, and smoking is banned in many public places such as offices, shops, restaurants, and bars. Many hotels are completely non-smoking and impose heavy fines on violators. The legal smoking age is 18.

T
Taxes
In San Francisco, a 9.5 percent sales tax is added to the price of all goods and services. Hotels charge a 15 percent tax that generally will not be included in quoted rates.

Telephones
Local calls are inexpensive; long-distance calls are not. Public phones accept coins and calling cards. The San Francisco area code is 415, which you only need to dial from outside the city; the country code is 1. Toll-free numbers begin 1-800, 1-888, 1-877, or 1-866.

Directory enquiries: 411.
US calls outside your area code: 1 +
area code + phone number.
International calls: 011+ country code
+ phone number.
Operator: 0 for assistance with local
calls; 00 for international calls.

Time Zones
San Francisco is on Pacific Standard
Time. PST is three hours behind
Eastern Standard Time (New York)
and eight hours behind Greenwich
Mean Time (London).

Tipping
Restaurants: 15-20 percent (even if
you were unsatisfied with the service
you should tip 10 percent). Most
restaurants add a service charge
automatically for parties of six or more.
Taxis: 10-15 percent.
Bars: 10-15 percent, or at least $1-2
per drink.
Coat check: $1-2 per coat.
Door attendants: $1-2 for hailing a
cab or bringing in bags.
Porters: $1-2 per bag.
Valet parking: $2-3.
Concierge: $5-10.
Maids: $3-5 per day.
Hairdressers and salons: 15-20
percent.

Tourist Information
**Visitor Information Center of San
Francisco:** 900 Market Street; tel: 391-
2000; www.onlyinsanfrancisco.com;

Nov–Apr Mon–Fri 9am–5pm, Sat 9am–
3pm (May–Oct also Sun 9am–3pm).
The center is down the stairway near
the cable-car turntable at Market and
Powell streets, and supplies brochures
and maps. Call for a listing of monthly
events (in multiple languages).

Transportation
A major hub for flights from all over the
world, San Francisco is easily reached
by air, while visitors from other parts
of the United States can opt to travel
by rail or bus. Once here, the city and
its outlying areas are comfortably
navigable by public transportation.

Getting to San Francisco
By Air
San Francisco International Airport
(SFO; 1 McDonnell Road; tel: 650-821-
8211; www.flysfo.com) is the major
international airport for northern
California. From Europe, all the major
airlines offer non-stop flights or
connections via New York, Chicago,
or Los Angeles. It also receives non-
stop, or one-stop, flights from all the
principal Pacific airports.

Despite being 13 miles away,
downtown San Francisco is easy to
reach. Taxis and shuttles line the inner
circle of the transportation zones of
the Arrivals/Baggage Claim Level,
while BART (Bay Area Rapid Transit),
located at the Departures/Ticketing
Level at the International Terminal and
accessible from the Domestic Terminal

by the Airtrain, takes passengers to downtown San Francisco and across the bay to various cities, for a minimal cost. The area is blanketed by Wi-Fi, which can be used for a fee.

The **Oakland International Airport** (OAK; 1 Airport Drive, Oakland; tel: 510-563-3300; www.flyoakland.com) is located 4 miles south of the city's downtown, and is accessible by BART. A hub for low-cost carriers, OAK is often a more economical alternative to the bigger and busier SFO.

The smallest of the three airports, **Mineta San Jose International Airport** (SJC; 1732 North 1st Street, San Jose; tel: 408-501-7600; www.sjc. org) is nearly 50 miles from downtown San Francisco.

By Train
While **Amtrak** (Emeryville depot, 5885 Horton Street, Emeryville; information line: 800-872-7245; www. amtrak.com), the cross-continental passenger rail line, does not connect directly to San Francisco, it has a free shuttle to deliver passengers to and from the depot in nearby Emeryville.

By Bus
The **Transbay Terminal** (425 Mission Street; information line: 800-231-2222; www.greyhound.com) is a major hub for the transcontinental **Greyhound** bus service.

The **Green Tortoise** (494 Broadway; information line: 800-8678-6473; www.

greentortoise.com; tel: 956-7500) is an alternative to Greyhound or Amtrak.

By Car
San Francisco is easy to reach by car. Interstates 101 and 80 pass through the city, while Interstates 5 and 99 are not too far away in the Central Valley. State Highway 1 runs along the coast of California and the western part of San Francisco.

Getting around San Francisco
For help navigating the entire Bay Area public transit system, including Muni buses and Metro streetcars, and BART *(see below)*, call 511 or look online at www.511.org; 511 offers assistance with planning trips using public transportation, traffic, and drive-time information.

BART (Bay Area Rapid Transit)
Fast and efficient, BART (www.bart. gov) allows passengers to get around the Bay Area in comfort. All BART lines travel through San Francisco, extending to San Francisco International Airport and under the bay to Oakland, Berkeley, and beyond. Stations provide maps that explain routes, fares, and automatic ticketing machines.

Four BART lines run through downtown and provide the quickest way to travel between downtown and the Mission district, or to reach Oakland and Berkeley.

Buses and Metro

Muni, the San Francisco Municipal Transit Agency, runs the city's orange-and-white diesel and electric buses, streetcars which run on lightrail lines underground through downtown, the historic F-line streetcars (comprising a collection of vintage trams from all over the world), and cable cars.

Purchasing a map is recommended and will make a stay in San Francisco infinitely simpler. They cost $2 and are available at the Muni kiosks at the Powell and Market, and Powell and Beach cable-car terminals, as well as in some stores where general maps are sold. They are also posted at many Muni Metro and bus stops.

For all Muni Metro and bus lines, adult fare is $2. Exact change is necessary, but transfers are given, allowing you to transfer different Muni Metro or bus lines within 90 minutes. Ride without limit on Muni-operated transport, including the cable cars, by using 1-, 3-, or 7-day visitor 'Passports.' They are sold at the baggage claim at San Francisco International Airport, on the mezzanine level of the Montgomery Muni Metro station, major cable-car terminals, and the kiosk at Bay and Taylor streets. For a list of other places where passes can be purchased and for route planning and general information, see www.sfmta. com. For up-to-the-minute information on when the vehicle you are waiting for will arrive, refer to www.nextmuni.com.

Cable Cars

Cable cars are also operated by Muni, but are the exception to most of the Muni rules. Fares can be purchased at the kiosk at each terminal or when you board. Drivers give exact change but not transfers.

Taxis

Taxis are a convenient but expensive way to get about when the majority of San Francisco's public transit shuts down around 12.30am. They hover around popular tourist or nightlife spots, but in out-of-the-way locations it is advisable to call a radio-dispatched taxi.

DeSoto Cab Company, tel: 970-1300
Green Cab, tel: 626-4733
Luxor Cab Company, tel: 828-4141
Yellow Cab, tel: 333-3333

Cycling

Around San Francisco, there are plenty of places to ride that are reasonably flat. Cycling through Golden Gate Park is a favorite, especially on Sundays, when many of the roads are vehicle-free. Bikes can be rented hourly or for the day, with rates varying by type of bike, but usually $20–60 per day and $7–10 per hour.

Driving

San Francisco is a difficult city in which to drive and park, often taxing the most experienced drivers. It is crisscrossed by one-way streets, and the fast-paced driving culture can easily unnerve any visitor. If it is necessary to rent a car, all the major car-rental companies have outlets at San Francisco International Airport and around the city.

Getting around the Bay Area
Caltrain
Caltrain (main San Francisco depot, 700 4th Street; information line: 800-660-4287; www.caltrain.org) runs alongside Highway 101 to San Jose, with limited extensions. It is largely a commuter train, but for visitors headed to the Peninsula or the South Bay, it is an enjoyable ride and accommodates passengers with bikes. Caltrain's terminus is near the AT&T Ballpark and many San Francisco Muni bus and Metro lines. Every Caltrain stop has an electronic ticket machine.

Ferries
Many locals use ferries for commuting, but for visitors they can provide a great scenic and environmental alternative to driving. Departing from Fisherman's Wharf or the Ferry Building, they travel to Angel Island and throughout the North and East Bay areas. Tickets can be purchased at the ticket windows next to the ferry terminals.
Blue and Gold Fleet, Pier 39 Marine Terminal, The Embarcadero at Beach Street; tel: 705-8200; www. blueandgoldfleet.com.
Golden Gate Ferry, Ferry Building,

The Embarcadero at Market Street; tel: 455-2000; www.goldengateferry.org.

Intercity Buses
Neighboring transit systems also connect San Francisco with other Bay Area cities. These buses can be caught downtown or at the Transbay Terminal.
Golden Gate Transit, Information line: 455-2000; www.goldengate.org.
Alameda Contra-Costa County Transit District, Information line: 510-891-4700; www.actransit.org.
San Mateo County Transit District, Information line: 510-817-1717; www. samtrans.org.

Visa Information
Visit the US Department of State web site (www.travel.state.gov) or tel: 202-663-1225 for information about visas.

Websites
Some helpful sites include:
www.sfgate.com (*San Francisco Chronicle*)
www.onlyinsanfrancisco.com (San Francisco Convention & Visitors Bureau)
www.sfist.com
www.fecalface.com/sf
www.friscomama.com
www.openwifispots.com for a list of hotels, cafes, and restaurants with WiFi.

Index

Insight Select Guide: San Francisco
Written by: Lisa Crovo Dion
Edited by: Tom Stainer
Layout by: Ian Spick
Maps: James Macdonald
Picture Manager: Steven Lawrence
Series Editor: Cathy Muscat
Photography: APA Ryan Pyle 46; Anomolous A
99; Alant 52; Alamy 30, 49, 50, 51, 65, 69, 70, 69,
71, 110, 111, 116, 121, 137, 155, 161; Hotel Argonaut
170M; Axiom 33, 149; Courtesy The Hotel Boheme
177T; Corbis 29; Dieseldemon 167; Lisa Dion 36,
37; Courtesy The Hotel Drisco 175T; Michael
Farjardo 118; Fotolibra 34/35, 117; Courtesy The
Sir Francis Drake 172M; Frankie Frankeny 9T;
Randal Gee 130; Courtesy The Garden Court Hotel
173M; Getty Images 86, 103, 164; Thomas Hawk
7T, 53, 57; Bill Holmes 72; Jeremy Hulebroeck 59;
Courtesy The Huntington Hotel 173; Courtesy The
Intercontinental 172B; Courtesy Jewish Museum
83; John Joh 140; Courtesy Kabuki Spa 104, 107T,
176M; Chris Kilkes 159; Madrone 17; Leonardo
172B; Luc Meir 141; Courtesy The Hotel Metropolis
170B; APA Abe Nowitz 8, 11, 22, 28, 31, 54/55, 73,
80/81, 82, 84, 85, 87, 92, 101, 124, 131, 142, 158, 160,
179B; APA Daniella Nowitz 3T, 4/5, 10B, 18T, 32,
40/41, 48, 60, 64, 70, 76, 88, 89, 90, 127, 128/129, 132,
136, 144/145, 146, 150, 154, 156/157, 174/175; APA
Richard Nowitz 2,3B, 6, 9B, 14, 10T, 13B/T, 15, 26,
47, 68, 74/75, 93, 94, 98, 100, 105, 108/109, 112, 122,
123, 125, 126, 148, 162, 165, 166, 171, 172M, 177B; PA
Photos 102, 106; Courtesy The Hotel Palomar 176B;
Courtesy The Phoenix Hotel; Photolibrary 27, 42;
Courtesy Pocket Opera 163; Precita Eyes Muralists
143; Courtesy The Red Victorian 174T; Courtesy
Hotel Rex 17M; Rex Features 18B; Courtesy Ritz
Carlton 171T; Jaqui Riviera 138; Courtesy The St
Regis 171B; Steve Silva 39; Blair Sneddon 139; Peter
Spier 14B, 120; Starwood Hotels 66, 173B; Erik
Tomason 91; Courtesy The Hotel Triton; When-
wedie 147; Courtesy The Washington Square Inn
178T; Courtesy The White Swan 178B; Brian Wolf
67; Teatro Zinzanni 38

First Edition 2010
© 2010 Apa Publications GmbH & Co.
Verlag KG Singapore Branch, Singapore.
Printed by CTPS-China
Distribution:
Distributed in the UK and Ireland by:
GeoCenter International Ltd
Meridian House, Churchill Way West, Basingstoke,
Hampshire RG21 6YR; tel: (44 1256) 817 987; email:
sales@geocenter.co.uk
Distributed in the United States by:
Langenscheidt Publishers, Inc.
36-36 33rd Street 4th Floor, Long Island City, New
York 11106; tel: (1 718) 784 0055; email: orders@
langenscheidt.com
Distributed in Australia by:
Universal Publishers
1 Waterloo Road, Macquarie Park, NSW 2113;
email: sales@universalpublishers.com.au
Distributed in New Zealand by:
Hema Maps New Zealand Ltd (HNZ)
Unit 2, 10 Cryers Road, East Tamaki, Auckland
2013; email: sales.hema@clear.net.nz
Worldwide distribution by:
Apa Publications GmbH & Co. Verlag KG
7030 Ang Mo Kio Ave 5, 08-65 Northstar @ AMK
Singapore 569880; tel: (65) 570 1051;
e-mail: apasin@singnet.com.sg
Contacting the Editors
We would appreciate it if readers would alert us to
outdated information by writing to:
Apa Publications, PO Box 7910, London SE1 1WE,
UK; email: insight@apaguide.co.uk

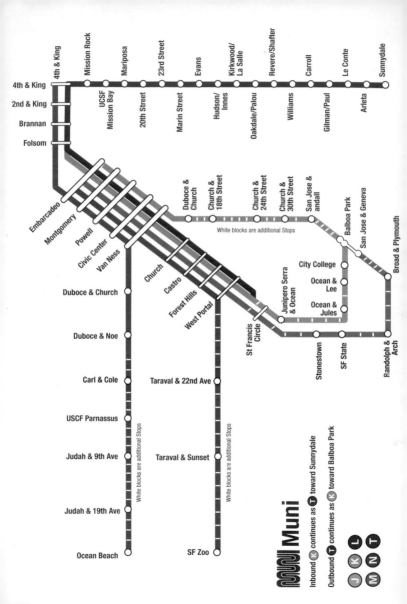

4th & King — Mission Rock, Mariposa, 23rd Street, Evans, Kirkwood/La Salle, Revere/Shafter, Carroll, Le Conte, Sunnydale

UCSF Mission Bay, 20th Street, Marin Street, Hudson/Innes, Oakdale/Palou, Williams, Gilman/Paul, Arleta

2nd & King
Brannan
Folsom

Embarcadeo
Montgomery
Powell
Civic Center
Van Ness

Church
Castro
Forest Hills
West Portal
St Francis Circle

Duboce & Church, Church & 18th Street, Church & 24th Street, Church & 30th Street, San Jose & andall

White blocks are additional Stops

Balboa Park
San Jose & Geneva
Broad & Plymouth

City College
Ocean & Lee
Ocean & Jules

Junipero Serra & Ocean

Duboce & Church
Duboce & Noe
Carl & Cole
USCF Parnassus
Judah & 9th Ave
Judah & 19th Ave
Ocean Beach

White blocks are additional Stops

Taraval & 22nd Ave
Taraval & Sunset
SF Zoo

White blocks are additional Stops

Stonestown
SF State
Randolph & Arch

Muni

Inbound **K** continues as **T** toward Sunnydale
Outbound **T** continues as **K** toward Balboa Park

L K N T
J M

192